FORBIDDEN KNOWLEDGE

OR IS IT...

D.A. MILLER

JOY PUBLISHING
P.O. Box 827
San Juan Capistrano, CA 92675

All Scriptures (spelling, punctuation and capitalization) taken from the King James Bible, Thru The Bible Edition, Thomas Nelson Press © 1976.

Front cover design by Nira
Typesetting by Diane Fillmore
Copyediting by Gina Renée Gross

Printed in the United States of America
10 9 8 7 6 5 4 3 2

Library of Congress Cataloging-in-Publication data

Forbidden Knowledge, Or Is It?
        by D. A. Miller

        1.Miller, Dorothy A. 2. Bible, Prophecy
Library of Congress Card # 91-76067
International Standard Book Number 0-939513-47-1

Published by
Joy Publishing
P.O. Box 827
San Juan Capistrano CA 92675

TABLE OF CONTENTS

PUBLISHER'S PREFACE

It is a rare occasion when an unfinished manuscript literally cries out to be published. *Forbidden Knowledge*, however, was one of those unusual manuscripts. In fact, it went to the top of the list of projects because of the urgency I felt for its message. Let me explain my reasons.

For many years, I had the concept that prophecy was something only "weirdos" studied and talked about. I distanced myself from anyone who discussed prophecy. Prophetic literature I came across seemed speculative and the speakers just added to the confusion.

Then I heard Chuck Missler, a radio Bible teacher. I listened as he revealed Scripture to me like no one ever had before. Soon, I realized that I had never heard these background details of Scripture. He showed that a very large part of the Bible is prophetic in nature. I came to see that the Bible could not be studied in its entirety without studying prophecy.

These in-depth insights began to make the Bible more clear to me. I gained a new desire to read God's Word. This interest in God's Word changed me from a man who tried to live in a Christian manner to a man who had a personal relationship with Jesus Christ.

That is why the manuscript was so important to me. The detailed background information presented in this book opens up the Scriptures in a special way. I pray that the Holy Spirit will lead you to truth and understanding.

Woody Young, Publisher

ACKNOWLEDGMENTS

Words cannot express my appreciation to the kind
friends (new and old) who used their time to read and
critique this book. God graciously spoke to me through
them. Their encouragement as well as their discerning
comments brought this book, *Forbidden Knowledge*, into
existence. Although I can offer no suitable recompense for
their assistance, my prayer is that our wonderful Lord will
greatly bless them for their contributions.

FOREWORD

Bible prophecy, especially eschatology (the study of "the last things"), has suffered greatly at the hands of both its enthusiasts and its detractors—the enthusiasts with their zeal for premature and unfounded conclusions; the detractors with their allegorizations and failure to regard the ancient texts with adequate diligence.

It is refreshing to experience a resurgence of interest in the literal and mystical aspects of the Scriptures. As a specialist in the information sciences for over thirty years, I have long been fascinated with the integrity of the Scriptures as a whole: sixty-six books, penned by forty authors over thousands of years—and yet evidencing an intricate design in which every textual detail, every number, every place name, all manifest careful design and diligent attention to detail.

It is in this very manner that this book explores some remarkable aspects of the Feasts of Israel—not just their historical basis and their commemorative role, but their prophetic role as well.

It is one of the tragedies of the historic Christian church that the widespread illiteracy with respect to the Tanakh (the Old Testament), as well as the general ignorance of "things Jewish," has masked from so many some of the amazing insights which God has hidden in the Torah (the first five books of Moses) with regards to His "Grand Design."

Furthermore, we have all been so badgered about the elusiveness of the "day and the hour" that we easily fall into the trap of being blindsighted by that which we can—and are instructed—to know.

Indeed, it is time for a fresh look.

Many of the perspectives and conjectures of the author will certainly meet with skepticism and disagreement, but this provocative study should challenge the reader to explore these insights further. After all, if we are "Children of the Day" (not of the Night) that day should *not* overtake *us* as a thief (1 Thessalonians 5:1–6).

Chuck Missler

INTRODUCTION

The Word of God is indeed alive and powerful. The Holy Spirit of God does teach those who prayerfully seek truth from the pages of Scripture.

This book reflects an eighteen-year struggle to adjust some of my prophetic beliefs to the Word of God. I had been taught, and I firmly believed, that although the general times and seasons of end-time events could be known from the Scriptures, "no one could know the day nor the hour."

Forbidden Knowledge questions this traditional theological interpretation of "the day and hour" and other Scriptures thought to prohibit exact dating of end-time events.

First you'll see in this book the amazing precision of God's prophetic information in the customs and feasts of Israel. Then, prompted by this enlightening information, you'll read a careful review of each Scripture and the traditional reasons that have kept us from believing we could know the "day and the hour."

SECTION I
PICTURES YES, BUT ARE THEY LABELED?

All Bible-believing Christians agree that prophecy is woven throughout the Scriptures. Everyone sees these pictures but how, specifically, does God reveal the timing of these events? Is the timing of some major events explained in the Scriptures while the arrival of others purposely hidden from our view?

In this section we will examine the "date setting" phenomenon of our day as well as gaze at one of the most beautiful prophetic pictures in the Bible.

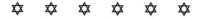

CHAPTER 1
DATE SETTERS ATTACK AGAIN

"Hear ye hear ye, Jesus is coming! Sell all that thou dost own and wait with the faithful on top of yonder mountain."

The faithful heard. They sold all their worldly goods, they traveled to yonder mountain, and they waited, and they waited, and they waited. Jesus did not come. Saddened and disillusioned, the followers lifted the hems of their white robes and descended the mountain amid the jeers of scoffing unbelievers.

Since the first century, when Jesus made His promise to return for those who placed their trust in Him, eager seekers have sought to discover the time of His arrival. Again and again earnest followers trusted in the projected dates only to be bitterly disappointed when Jesus did not appear.

A typical example of this phenomenon grew from the teachings of William Miller. He made his splash in the pond of prophetic history by predicting Christ's visible return in 1843, but later postponed the date to October 22, 1844. Thousands of eager followers of this guide sold all their belongings, gathered together on the special date, and waited in zealous anticipation. Those vying for the front row "climbed to the tops of trees,"[1] presumably so they would be taken first. Great disillusionment followed when the day came and left without the appearing of Christ.

Reactions to Predictions

Looking back over the centuries at the disheartened folks, who trusted the wisdom of numerous predictions, brings sadness. This sadness comes first from the realization that scores of people blindly followed the "enlightened" understanding of a prophetic interpreter. Often, these predictors used only the troubled events of their times as the basis for their chosen "apocalyptic" dates. Also heartbreaking are the many unbiblical **reactions** to belief in the soon coming of their Savior. One has to ask what **climbing a tree** has to do with meeting our beloved Jesus Christ?

Certainly, if at any time God actually had revealed the day of Jesus' Second Coming, the believer's reactions should have been ones of deeper commitment to serving Christ, conforming to His image, and telling others of His saving grace. Their often bizarre withdrawal from society and clinging to one another demonstrates a lack of searching the Scriptures for "the whole counsel of God." Soberly, in this twentieth century, we viewed the Jonestown massacre as an ultimate illustration of these bizarre reactions. The tragic death of nine hundred people resulted from a compelling desire to follow a leader rather than personally to search the Scriptures for truth.

Twentieth Century Rise in Predictions

As we near the end of the twentieth century, a rise in "doomsday setting" is again being heard. This increase in "date setting" is familiar. Historically, mankind has endeavored to tie in biblical prophecy with the calendar and with world events. However, this effort always seems to increase toward the end of every century as well as during times of disaster and social upheavals.

The editors of *The Encyclopedia of Religion* list one idea for this rise in "end time" interest: "The historical myth[a] persists because it seems to many that the year 2000 will be truly millennial. The discovery of the Dead Sea Scrolls since 1947 has underscored the contention, popularized by Albert Schweitzer in 1906, that escatological[b] hope was vital at the time of apostolic Christianity and should therefore be a part of all true Christian belief. Israel's statehood in 1948 and its 1967 reunification of Jerusalem have convinced fundamentalist Christians of the nearness of the Second Coming, for which a principal sign is the Jew's return to Zion."[2]

Time magazine states that its senior writer, Otto Friedrich, refers to this phenomenon in a book he authored. "In his meditation on history, *The End of the World*, solemn predictions of earth's final days have accompanied natural and man-made catastrophes down through the ages, from the sack of Rome to the Nazi Holocaust. This century's military technology has given new power to those primoral fears and illusions."[3]

"The world is headed for 'Apocalypse soon'" begins a story in *US News and World Report*. The article relates the swelling sound of prophetic voices prompted by world events, particularly in the Middle East. "This isn't just the talk of a handful of charlatans, exhorting naive followers to sell their possessions and flee to the mountains. It is a message increasingly being heard from the pulpits and airwaves of mainstream Christian evangelists and resonantly striking a chord among tens of thousands of conservative Christians." This writer continues by mentioning Billy Graham's warning that "there are 'spiritual forces at work' in

---

[a] From this description of the biblical teaching of the Millennium, one must assume this editor lives with no expectancy of the coming of Jesus.

[b] Study of last or final things, particularly related to the Bible.

the Persian Gulf confrontation. 'History has gone full circle, and we are coming back to these [Bible] lands.'"[4]

Indeed, the twentieth century has been saturated with predictions of impending doom, messiahs and utopian world peace. The seventies and the eighties encountered a large share of selected dates which passed with no fulfillments. The nineties promise an explosion of prophetic forecasts.

How strange that although theologians point to specific Scriptures that forbid the knowledge of an exact date, a minority of curious seekers continue to search for this "forbidden" information.

Although respected Christian theologians, since the time of Christ, have not agreed on every detail concerning the Second Coming of Christ and the end of the world, they have concurred in one area. They have agreed that the **exact timing** of the coming of Jesus is hidden from mankind by God. Of course, cited as proof are the words of Jesus, *"No man knoweth the day and the hour."*[c]

Why Do They Continue?

One does wonder why these date setters continue their hunt amid the flack coming from both conservative and liberal Christians as well as the secular world. Are they deluded? Aren't they aware of Scriptures that expressly prohibit this kind of search? Do they have any biblical ground on which to stand or are they, as some critics suggest, simply sensationalists seeking to sell books or to be noticed?

Sincere Christians know that the Bible contains many exact prophecies. The existence of prophecy is not in question but we must follow scriptural guidelines to

---

[c] Matthew 24:36; Mark 13:32

determine the extent that **future prophetic events** can be understood. Because of the torrent of prophetic teaching flooding over us during the end of the twentieth century, we must deal with this "dating" trend. In an effort not to damage members of the Christian body, this analysis will be done by carefully examining biblical prophecies both past and future rather than challenging individual teachers.

Prophetic Pictures

The exactness of the fulfilled prophecies concerning the first coming of Jesus (His birth, life, death, and Resurrection) have convinced Christians throughout the ages that Jesus is indeed the Messiah prophetically described in the pages of the Old Testament. Since the New Testament (as well as most of the Old) was written by Jews, much of our inquiry about prophetic events will be done from a Jewish perspective.

We will look particularly at the following question concerning the timing of future events: Since Scripture foretold precise details concerning the **first** coming of Jesus, can we expect Scriptures to reveal future world events and the timing of Jesus' **second** appearance?

This book will reveal precise information concerning future events. More importantly, it will offer scriptural freedom to look for exact times of end-time events.

In the past, followers of soothsayers reacted to prophecy in an unbiblical manner. As we hear prophecy taught today and as we consider the suggestions in this book, we must react as did the Bereans whom God commended. They knew that when anyone claimed to possess information from God, the information must be examined in light of the Scriptures as to "*whether those things were so.*"[d]

As obedient Christians in a world of darkness we also must individually "*study to show thyself approved unto God, a workman that needeth not to be ashamed, rightly dividing the word of truth,*"[e] and "*be ready to answer every man that asketh a reason of the hope that is in you, with meekness and fear.*"[f] We must insure that each scriptural interpretation we embrace comes from the teaching of the Holy Spirit, not just from opinions of men. At times it's tempting to rely on the studies and viewpoints of those whom we respect, as if these mortals knew all truth. However, we must continually remind ourselves that God holds each **individual** accountable for "*rightly dividing the word of truth.*"[g]

Historic Messianic Anticipation

The belief in the soon-coming of Christ permeated Christian belief throughout the first three centuries after Christ. According to historical records, James, the half brother of Jesus, declared just before his execution, "Jesus is about to come on the clouds of heaven."

The Encyclopedia of Religious Ethics records that noted believers, Ignatius and Polycarp, believed themselves to be living in the last times. They expected Christ to suddenly appear, executing judgment upon the persecutors of Christians and rewarding the faithful.

---

[d] Acts 17:10, 11

[e] II Timothy 2:15

[f] I Peter 3:15

[g] II Timothy 2:15

One of the early apologists[h], Justin, thought that Christ might delay His Second Coming temporarily to allow more sinners to repent, "even long enough to include some who are not yet born."

One leader in the early church, Irenaeus, agreed with the Epistle of Barnabas "in placing the end of the world and the return of Christ six thousand years after creation."[5]

A falling away in the belief of a literal Second Coming and actual "one-thousand-year" reign of peace by Jesus Christ resulted from Origen's introduction of an allegorical interpretation to the Scriptures. This approach to Scripture stifled interest in prophetic study and produced doubt in the relevancy and inspiration of the prophetic portions of the Bible. Until after the eleventh century, a wilful neglect of prophecy dominated the larger organizations of those who called themselves Christians.

Historically, just a few scattered students of the prophetic Scriptures maintained a belief in the literal, imminent return of Jesus. However just before the year 1000, a surge of interest flowed across Christian groups. Researchers tell us, that leading theologian, Augustine's "identification of the Church with the ideal earthly kingdom of Christ implied that the millennium would close about A.D. 1000, and that the final coming of Christ in judgment might be expected. The approach of this date awakened a revival of interest in Second Advent hopes and for several years thereafter more or less vivid expectations were frequently entertained."[6]

In the article "Millennial Madness," Ron Rhodes refers to people caught up in this wave of millennial prospect. "Prisoners were freed yet many remained, wishing to expiate their sins before the end. As Christmas (A.D. 999) arrived, there was an outpouring of love. Stores gave away food;

---

[h]   A person involved in systematic defense of the divine origin and authority of Christianity.

merchants refused payment. On December 31 the frenzy reached new heights."[7]

Sadly, as the year rolled over into 1000 with no appearance of Christ, life soon returned to normal. The euphoria of love towards one another gave way once more to a climate of self-centered existence.

From the twelfth to the twentieth centuries, eager but mistaken predictors of "end-time" dates bobbed to prominence. Each date stirred faithful, but perhaps gullible, followers. In some instances the promoters of these projected dates admonished their adherents to live in purity to prepare for the soon-expected arrival of Jesus. More commonly, however, devoted followers were deluded by these convincing "prophets" to forsake all their worldly goods and gather at some lofty or secluded place where they, "the faithful," would be the only ones invited to rise to meet the expected Savior.

Throughout history many of these seekers committed themselves to the prediction of an **exact day** for the coming of Christ! A few of the well-known predictions are:[8]

1. Joachim of Flores gave A.D. 1260 as the expected return of Christ. He based this on the 1260 days listed in Revelation 12. The Crusades and other cataclysms of his day fueled a belief in this date.

2. Militz of Kromeriz was more conservative. His date rested somewhere from 1365 to 1367.

3. Scottish mathematician, John Napier, wisely gave space in his prediction. He expected the "End" somewhere between 1688 and 1700.

4. Joseph Mede used information from Revelation to select 1660 as the close of history.

5. Pierre Jurieu of France "sought to comfort the Huguenots by predicting the downfall of the Antichrist Roman Church in the year 1689."[9]

6. William Whitson boldly gave 1715, which he changed to 1734, which he then changed to 1866!

7. J.A. Bengal concluded that a preliminary millennium would be inaugurated in 1836.

8. Joseph Smith, well-known founder of the Mormon church (Jesus Christ Church of The Latter-Day Saints), told his followers in 1830 that God had chosen him to found a community that would constitute a present city of Zion. This city would be ready for Christ when He set up His millennial kingdom.[10]

9. Joseph Worlf "began prophesying that Jesus would come to the mount of Olives in 1847. English traveller, Lady Hester Stanhope, converted to his doctrine, moved to Palestine, and established residence on the Mount of Olives. She kept two beautiful white Arabian horses in stables there. One was for Jesus to ride through the Golden Gate."[11]

10. C.T. Russell was the last great predictor of the nineteenth century. He declared 1874 as the definite date for the return

of Christ and announced 1914 as the end of the world. This predictor's present-day disciples, known as Jehovah's Witnesses, now take the posture that the prophesied, literal return of Jesus Christ actually took place in 1914 but only the faithful saw Him!

11. Probably the most widely publicized of the twentieth century dates is September 11 −13, 1988. Edgar C. Whisenant was adamant in his book, *88 Reasons The Rapture Could Be in 1988*, about the selection of these days for the Rapture of the Christian Believers. Not to be overlooked, other less outspoken prophecy teachers also placed their apples in this same-dated basket. Although some vigilant Christians immediately and openly criticized these teachers for "date setting," most of the critics waited until after the date passed with no Rapture or appearance of Jesus before they literally piggy-backed one another to ridicule the "soothsayers."

Christians Aren't the Only Predictors

Even Jewish religious leaders are picking up on the end-time fervor. This anticipation involves genuine belief that the temple must be rebuilt now, in preparation for the soon-coming Messiah. A group of Jews faithfully prepares implements to furnish the expected temple, while others fashion proper priestly garb for the qualified Kohens[i] who currently train for temple service.

---

[i] Descendants of Aaron from the Jewish Tribe of Levi.

Some Jews actually busy themselves locating solid red-haired cows. Biblical law requires the sacrifice of a "red heifer" for the cleansing ceremony[j] in order for temple service to be legally reinstated. Other searchers dedicated to this soon-to-come messianic time are frantically exploring special caves in Israel to try and locate the original ashes of the Red Heifer and other authentic temple artifacts. They believe that an ancient copper scroll, found in cave number eight, specifically describes a cave where the temple treasures were hidden just before the destruction of the temple in A.D. 70.

Some searchers also believe these caves might be the location of the original Ark of the Covenant while others give convincing reasons why the Ark might be located in Ethiopia.[12]

The messianic fervor is fanned by reports such as this one in *The Jerusalem Post*. "Rebbe Menahem Schneerson, a beloved Lubavicher leader, stated in August of 1990, 'This year, according to a Midrash (a homiletical[k] interpretation of the Scripture), there will be great ferment between the different states, and then a confrontation in the Gulf that will shake the world. **Then Messiah will come,** stand on the roof of the temple, and announce to Israel: The time of your redemption has come.'"[13]

"What is going on in Iraq is definitely **a sign of the imminent arrival of the Messiah,**" quoted the *Miami Herald* of Rabbi Mendel Fogelman, a leader of the Israeli branch of the dynamic, modern, and yet fundamentalist, Chabad movement.[l]

---

[j] Numbers 8:6, 7, 19:1-22

[k] Teaching through preaching.

[l] Martin Merzer, *The Miami Herald*, September 7, 1990.

Although the messianic fervor is building in the nineties, Rabbi Professor Leon Askhenazi, a Jerusalem-based Sephardi scholar, believes, "One does not just get up and start believing in a Messianic Era just because of what happens this year. I believe that the process was underway a long time ago, because the advent of Zionism signified the Ingathering of the Exiles."

Some projections for the messianic movement, mentioned in the *Post* article, include ideas such as "using 1917 and the Balfour Declaration as the starting point for the Ingathering of the Exiles." Askhenazi states, "The Book of Daniel predicted that fifty years after the Ingathering, Jerusalem will be reunified (1967), to be followed twenty-five years later by the reconstruction of the temple."

Askhenazi "acknowledges the dangers of over-enthusiasm in making conclusions based on today's headlines. Yet he notes certain pre-messianic parallels: the war occurring at the same time as the massive Soviet/Ethiopian Aliya (the Ingathering of the Exiles) and America's role in the Gulf (there is a biblical passage noting that others will do Israel's work for her **prior to the arrival of the Messiah.**"[14]

Our Search for Prophetic Truth

First, we will once again savor the beautiful Bible prophecies, that led to the first coming of Jesus.

We then will examine some of the many Scriptures that give us information concerning His Second Coming and the end of our present world system.

Lastly, we will review the Scriptures used to prove a biblical prohibition concerning "exact dating" of end-time events.

Most of all, as we look at this exciting information, let us thrill together as we view wondrous prophetic pictures painted by God using the brush of Jewish life.

CHAPTER 2
WHERE IS MANKIND HEADED AND WHEN?

Are events in the Middle East leading to some type of Armageddon? If so, does God give any information in the Bible as to when these world-shattering events might occur? Does God tell us when the Rapture and the end of the world will be?

Before we answer these specific questions from a biblical perspective, let's look back at a group of worried men living during the time of Christ on earth. These men, disciples of Jesus, had questions about their futures, much the same as we do. The truth that Jesus would soon be leaving, struck panic to their hearts.

Jesus in His usual calm manner comforts His followers by saying, *"Let not your hearts be troubled: ye believe in God, believe also in me. In my father's house are many mansions: if it were not so I would have told you. I go to prepare a place for you, and if I go to prepare a place for you, I will come again and receive you unto myself; that where I am, there ye may be also. And whither I go ye know and the way ye know."*

Thomas, who became famous for his habit of verbalizing his doubts, pleads, *"Master, we know not whither thou goest; and how can we know the way?"*

"Jesus saith unto him, I am the way, the truth, and the life, no man cometh unto the Father, but by me."[a]

To understand the full impact of these words on His disciples we must look into the customs of the times. In so doing we will realize the great calming influence these words must have had on His worried followers.

In fact, for nineteen hundred years, millions of readers have been inspired by the words and stories of Jesus written in the four Gospels of the New Testament. Jesus, here in His soothing words to the disciples, had alluded to the marriage customs of the day.

Jewish Weddings

Throughout the New Testament, God uses the analogy of a bride and groom to describe the relationship of Jesus to the church.[b] As a groom pledged love to his bride, so Jesus committed His love to believers, pledged to return for us and promised us an eternity spent with Him.[c]

The people of Jesus' day fully understood the betrothal[d] and marriage customs of which He spoke. However, we in the twentieth century need to look at these ceremonies as they were during the first century, to fully understand the significance of Jesus' teachings. This understanding not only deepens our appreciation of God's love for us, it also gives us added insights to prophetic events and offers comfort in a time of world unrest.

---

[a] John 14:1-6

[b] A New Testament term for believers in Jesus Christ. Ephesians 5:23-33.

[c] John 14:1-6; Ephesians 5:23-32; Revelation 19:7-9, 21:9 and 22:17

[d] A pre-marriage agreement similar to engagement.

Jewish Weddings First-Century Style

When a Jewish young man wished to marry a particular young woman, it was customary for the prospective groom's father first to approach the girl's father with the proposal of marriage. The two men would discuss this possible union including the price[e] offered by the groom for the bride. If the girl's father agreed to the suggested amount, the two men sealed the agreement with a toast of wine.

The potential bride then entered the room whereupon the prospective groom proclaimed his love and asked her to be his bride. If the young woman wished to be his wife, she accepted his proposal at this time. The validation of the agreement made by the engaged couple was the presentation of a gift by the groom. He offered it in the presence of at least two witnesses. As he gave the gift, usually a ring, he said to his intended bride, "Behold you are consecrated unto me with this ring according to the laws of Moses and Israel."

Arrangements were also made right then concerning the terms of the marriage. A written contract listed the time, place, and size of the wedding as well as recording the dowry and terms of maintenance of the marriage. This binding document called a "ketubah" was kept in the bride's possession until the consummation of the marriage.[15] Finally, this first part of a two-part ceremony was concluded by the toast of a glass of wine.[16] The whole ceremony was called the "Shiddukhin,"[f] or engagement.

The Bible refers to the status of the prospective bride and groom as "espousal" or "betrothal." It meant that the two

---

[e] The price paid by the groom was called a dowry.

[f] This Jewish word and others, as well as theological terms, are listed for reference in the glossary.

people were committed to each other as much as a married couple would be. The only parts of the marriage not yet completed were the formal "huppah" ceremony followed by their physical union. This betrothal was considered so binding that the only way to break it was by an actual bill of divorcement.[17]

The groom then departed, but not before he assured his bride with the promises of building a home for her and returning to complete the marriage ceremony. He usually took a year to prepare her new home which often consisted of an addition built onto his own father's house.[18]

The bride was expected to remain true to her groom as she prepared herself and her trousseau. She lived for the day of his return for her which would be heralded by a shout from the members of the wedding party. The impending return of her groom was to influence the bride's behavior during this interim espousal period.

The typical Jewish wedding took place at night.[19] As soon as any members of the wedding spotted the moving torches signaling the groom's approach, their cry echoed through the streets, "The bridegroom is coming." The *Wycliffe Bible Encyclopedia* tells us, "Mirth and gladness announced their approach to townspeople waiting in houses along the route to the bride's house."[20] Upon hearing the announcement, the excited bride would drop everything in order to slip into her wedding dress and complete her final personal preparations for marriage.

Rather than the groom entering the bride's house, the bride came out to meet him. The two, accompanied by their wedding party, returned together to the groom's home for the marriage ceremony. Following the public ceremony, the newlyweds entered their bridal chamber to be intimate with each other for the first time. After this union, the groom came out and announced to the wedding guests, "Our marriage is consummated."

Upon receiving the glad news, the wedding party began a "festive" seven-day celebration. The celebration lasted seven days only if this was the first marriage of a virgin girl.[21] During this time the bride and the groom stayed with each other in seclusion. At the end of this time of privacy, the groom would present his unveiled bride to everyone in attendance. The newlyweds then joined in the wedding feast with the guests.

Jesus the Groom, Believers the Bride

In the Bible, God describes mankind by such unflattering examples as dumb sheep, foolish builders, temporary grass, vipers, ornate tombs, and blind leaders of the blind. Of course these and other disparaging descriptions fit us all too well. But, because of God's great love, He has other, quite compassionate ways to describe His feelings toward those who respond to His offer of salvation. He gives us such wonderful titles as, Sons, Joint Heirs with Christ, Beloved, and Children. One of the most tender terms used to describe us is "the bride, the Lamb's Wife."[g]

We just reviewed customs surrounding first-century Jewish betrothals and weddings. Now let's explore how these might relate to us as Christians today. Then let's seek to uncover the possible prophetic information presented in these ceremonies.

In eternity past, God the Father and God the Son planned our salvation.[h] The Bible states concerning God, *"He hath chosen us in him before the foundation of the world."*[i] They settled the price long before the offer of salvation was

---

[g] Revelation 21:9

[h] Psalm 110:1-4

[i] Ephesians 1:4

given to us. We see God the Father as the "father of the groom" and because Jesus is actually the creative person of the Godhead,ⁱ He stands in as the "the father of the bride."

How encouraging to realize this offer of love was not an afterthought of God. In fact, the Scripture refers to Jesus as *"the lamb slain from the foundation of the world."*ᵏ

Jesus (in the form of a man) also steps into the role of the prospective groom. He offered **Himself** as the "price" for us, His intended bride. God actually says about us, *"For ye are bought with a price."*ˡ

After the plan was established, this loving proposal of salvation was given by Jesus to all mankind. God explains that everyone has the opportunity to respond to His offer. The Bible says, *"For whosoever shall call upon the name of the Lord shall be saved." "The heavens declare the glory of God and the firmament sheweth his handywork...There is no speech nor language where their voice is not heard."* God also warns us that everyone understands who He is, so when people reject this proposal of love they are *"without excuse."*ᵐ

When we answer "yes" to Jesus' offer of marriage, we become His betrothed. This arrangement is secured by the Holy Spirit, who protects the purchased bride until the return of Jesus. God says, *"Ye were sealed with the Holy Spirit of promise, which is the earnest of our inheritance until the redemption of the purchased possession, unto the praise of his glory."*ⁿ Our "engagement ring" of promise is none other than the Holy Spirit of God Himself.

ⁱ Colossians 1:12-18

ᵏ Revelation 13:8

ˡ I Corinthians 6:19, 20

ᵐ Romans 10:13; Psalm 19:1, 3; Romans 1:18-20

ⁿ Ephesians 1:13, 14

Imagine too, that just as the Jewish bride of long ago held the written promise of marriage commitment (Ketubah) in her hand, so the prospective bride of Christ today holds the Bible in her hands. These written promises from Jesus describe his everlasting love and commitment.

On the night before His Crucifixion, Jesus drank a glass of wine with His followers. Lifting the cup He declared, "*This cup is the New Testament in my blood, which is shed for you.*" Paul reminds us that Jesus commanded, "*This do ye, as oft as ye drink it, in remembrance of me.*"[o] Just as the groom in a Jewish marriage toasted his espoused bride, so we, by the communion cup, remember our betrothal to Jesus and the supreme price He paid for us.

Jesus said He must leave us in order to go back to His Father's house and prepare our new home. He promised also to return and gather all those who constitute His bride and transport them to this new home.[p] This parallels exactly the ancient marriage customs!

For nearly two thousand years, Jesus has been in heaven "preparing a place for us." In God's time, Jesus will "*descend from heaven with a shout, with the voice of the archangel, and with the trump of God... We which are alive and remain shall be caught up together with them in the clouds to meet the Lord in the air: so shall we ever be with the Lord.*"[q] This catching away, called by many "the Rapture," is pictured in the Jewish marriage custom. The groom comes to the bride's home and brings her back to the wedding ceremony which is held at his father's house. This is the same house where he has also prepared a home for her.

---

[o] Luke 22:20, I Corinthians 11:25

[p] John 14:1-3

[q] I Thessalonians 4:16, 17

Although we, the bride of Christ, have known for nearly two thousand years that Jesus would return for us, we have only been able to say, "He's coming back—maybe in my lifetime." *"For our conversation is in heaven; from whence we look also for the Savior, the Lord Jesus Christ."*[r]

We have, of necessity, spent a portion of our lives involved in mundane matters since we didn't know the exact time of His return. However, just as the first-century bride reacted excitedly when she heard the shout across town announcing the impending arrival of her groom, so we as the listening bride of Christ should react when we hear the call, ahead of Jesus' arrival, "The bridegroom is coming."

The wedding celebration of seven days is carried on by the guests while the bride and groom spend this time in seclusion. At the end of the seven days the groom brings his bride out and her veil is removed for the first time, so all the guests can see her beauty.

This is a picture of the seven-year celebration in heaven which occurs simultaneously with the seven year time of Tribulation transpiring on earth. The culmination of this time is described in the Bible. *"Let us be glad and rejoice, and give honor to him: for the marriage of the Lamb is come, and his wife hath made herself ready. And to her was granted that she should be arrayed in fine linen, clean and white: for the fine linen is the righteousness of the saints. And he saith unto me, Write, Blessed are they which are called unto the marriage supper of the Lamb."*[s]

John Walvoord writes that "the marriage symbolism is beautifully fulfilled in the relationship of Christ to His Church. Revelation 19:6–9 is actually a prophetic hymn anticipating the marriage of the Lamb and His bride after He has begun His reign, and He will not begin His reign on

---

[r] Philippians 3:20

[s] Revelation 19:7-9

earth until He has conquered the kings of the earth led by Antichrist."[22]

The Jewish wedding, a perfect picture from beginning to end of Jesus' love for believers, should melt our hearts with appreciation. The prophetic picture is quite accurate, bringing us once again to see that God has woven many time clues in the Scriptures for us to discover.

✿ ✿ ✿ ✿ ✿ ✿

SECTION II
FEAST DAYS

Other prophetic pictures of Jesus exist in Scripture besides this one in the marriage ceremony. Let's not overlook these lesser-known prepictures. By gaining knowledge of the Jewish life and customs that weave through the whole fabric of the Bible, we can discover magnificent portrayals of Jesus in this Hebrew tapestry.

From Genesis to Revelation, God has embroidered pictures of Jesus in Scripture that foretell His original coming as Messiah (called the Incarnation), His snatching away of the believers (known as the Rapture), and His return to reign on earth (called His Second Coming).

A particularly exciting realm of prophecy is found in the Jewish feast days. Throughout history, numerous spiritual events have occurred on these pre-established Jewish Holy days. These events not only occurred on Jewish celebration days, but they also typify the meaning of the celebrations. The timing and message of these fulfillments correspond so well to the earlier celebrations, that Bible students realize the match-ups are not accidental.

These non-coincidental similarities demonstrate the principle of **veiled information being hidden in the Feast days.** Colossians 2:16–17 verifies this concept. "*Let no man therefore judge you in meat or in drink, or of the new moon, or of the sabbath days: <u>Which are a shadow of things to come</u>.*" This principle obligates students of the Bible to pursue a deeper understanding of these God-given festivals. Another Scripture describing the principle of hidden information being typified in Old Testament Jewish ordinances is, *"priests...who serve unto the example and the shadow of heavenly things."*[a]

God gives us a complete list of the seven Jewish feasts in Leviticus, chapter 23. In verse two, God says to Moses, *"Speak unto the children of Israel, and say unto them, Concerning the feasts of the Lord, which ye shall proclaim to be holy convocations, even these are my feasts."*

It is noteworthy, as brought out by Coulson Shepherd in *Jewish Holy Days*,[23] that the meaning of the Hebrew word "mowar" translated "feasts"[b] carries the thought, "to keep an appointment." It also ties in with our study to note the Hebrew word "miqraw" translated "holy convocation," means "a public meeting or a rehearsal."

Perhaps these feasts are pictures of God's appointments with mankind. Could these holy convocations, given to the Jews, actually be rehearsals of future great events on God's calendar?

Using the premise that all of the Old Testament ordinances have a New Testament and/or prophetic importance, let's explore the seven feasts mandated by God to the Jews.

---

[a] Hebrews 8: 4,5

[b] Hebrew word "mowed." *Strong's Exhaustive Concordance of the Bible*, Hebrew Lexicon Section, entry #4150, an appointment or fixed time.

The Jewish Calendar

By Jewish months, the seven feasts in Leviticus 23 are:

FEAST	JEWISH MONTH	HEBREW WORD
1. PASSOVER	Nisan 14 (falls in April or May)	Pesach
2. UNLEAVENED BREAD	Nisan 15	Hag-Ha-Matzot
3. FIRSTFRUITS	It begins "on the morrow after the Sabbath"[c] following Passover.	Bikkurim
4. FEAST OF WEEKS	It begins fifty days after Firstfruits. (falls in May or June)	Shavuot
5. FEAST OF TRUMPETS	Tishri 1 (September or October)	Rosh HaShanah
6. DAY OF ATONEMENT	Tishri 10	Yom Kippur
7. FEAST OF TABERNACLES	Tishri 15	Succoth

---

[c] Sabbath is the Hebrew word "to stop, or cease from labor." It is the name of the Jewish seventh day of the week which corresponds with the Gentile calendar days of Friday night and Saturday daylight hours. The word Sabbath is also used to describe some special holy days in the Bible.

The God-given dates of these feasts offer enlightenment concerning both the original and prophetic meanings of the feasts. These dates seem confusing at first since the Jewish calendar is uniquely different from all other calendars. This difference comes because the Hebrew calendar is determined by the moon's position, while the Gentile or Gregorian calendar is based on the movement of the sun.

The two different systems cause the Gregorian calendar dates to correspond only generally with the Hebrew calendar dates, thus making exact comparison difficult.

God originally designated Nisan (Abib) as the first month of the Hebrew calendar.[24] This sequence became known as the religious calendar. Later the Jews introduced a civil calendar which instituted the month of Tishri as the first month of the year causing Tishri 1 to become the Jewish "New Year's Day."

Two Ways of Beginning a "Day"

One other important facet of the Jewish calendar system is the distinctive time a new day is started. A new day is declared on the exact moment of sundown (approximately 6:00 P.M.). This system of day counting is based on the creation story as outlined in Genesis chapter 1 which defines each day as "evening and morning." Of course this is in contrast to the Gregorian or Gentile system which begins each new day at 12:00 midnight.

The following chart shows the months of both calendars, the occurrences of the feast days, and how they correspond in the years 1992–1995. Notice the way the feasts occur on different days of the month in the Gregorian versus the Jewish calendar.

CALENDAR YEAR OF FEASTS
(sample as celebrated by Jews today)

LUNAR JEWISH CALENDAR Feasts and Months in Hebrew		SOLAR GREGORIAN CALENDAR Feasts and Months in English				
			1992	1993	1994	1995
Pesach	Nisan 14	Passover	April 18	April 6	March 27	April 15
Hag-Ha-Matzot	Nisan 15	Unleavened Bread	April 19	April 7	March 28	April 16
Bikkurim	Nisan 16	Firstfruits	April 20	April 8	March 29	April 17
	Iyar					
Shavout	Silvan 50th day after Firstfruits	Feast of Weeks	June 7	May 26	May 16	June 4
	Tamuz					
	Av					
	Elul					
Rosh HaShanah	Tishri 1	Trumpets	September 28	September 16	September 6	September 25
Yom Kippur	Tishri 10	Atonement Day	October 7	September 25	September 15	October 4
Succoth	Tishri 15	Tabernacles	October 12	September 30	September 20	October 9

The first three feasts are grouped close together in the first month, then the fourth feast is fifty days later. Next, there is a gap of almost four months, and then the last three feasts follow in the seventh month.

Everything God does, everything recorded in His word, is exactly what He wants to convey to mankind. The numbers, the dates, the stories; all have been designed and recorded for His purposes. Jesus says, *"One jot or one tittle[d] shall in no wise pass from the law, till all be fulfilled."[e]*

Let's view the significance the feast days held for the Jews, then scrutinize the feasts for prophetic importance.

---

[d] Smallest symbols in Hebrew writing

[e] Matthew 5:18

CHAPTER 3
PASSOVER (Feast #1)

SPRING
NISAN 14
Preparation for Passover

The descendants of Abraham, Isaac, and Jacob constitute the nation of Israel. In fact, Jacob's name was changed to Israel by God. God promised all three of these progenitors that their descendants would own the land of Canaan forever. During a severe famine, when this clan numbered only seventy, Pharaoh invited them to move into Egypt. Later, because the Jews multiplied to a respectable-size nation, the Egyptians (fearing an internal take-over) forced the Israelites into slavery.

God warned Pharaoh in Exodus, chapter 4, *"Thus saith the Lord, Israel is my son, even my firstborn; And I say unto thee Let my son go, that he may serve me; and if thou refuse to let him go, I will slay thy son even thy firstborn."* Then through nine successive plagues,[25] God continued to ask Pharaoh to release His people to go into the desert on a three-day journey to offer sacrifice unto the Lord. Pharaoh acquiesced, agreeing to their release in order to cause each plague to stop, but then nine times he changed his mind and refused to let them go.

Ultimately, God's message came that He would indeed kill the firstborn of every family in Egypt. This last judgment devastated Pharaoh, and finally caused him to release the Jewish slaves for their time of worship.

Amazingly, God had given their revered ancestor Abraham the details of this migration, slavery, and exact time of release.[a]

The feast of Passover commemorates this time in Egypt when the Lord spared the lives of the firstborn Jews. God literally "passed over" the homes of those who had believed and obeyed His instructions for safety.

Through Moses, God had instructed the Jews that on the tenth day of Nisan each household must select a male lamb without blemish. They obeyed God, and after carefully selecting their lambs to insure perfection, they killed them on the fourteenth day of this first month. God also commanded, "*Neither shall ye break a bone thereof.*" They were instructed to "*take of the blood and strike it on the two side posts and on the upper door post of the houses.*" God explained how they must roast the meat and eat it along with unleavened bread and bitter herbs. None of the sacrificed lamb could remain until the morning.[b] He finished the outline of Passover by commanding the Jews to commemorate their release from bondage by celebrating this feast every year at the same time.

According to Jewish scholars, this passover meal,[c] as outlined in the Torah,[d] was repeated every year on the

---

[a] Genesis 15:13-16

[b] Exodus 12:1-13; Leviticus 23:4, 5

[c] Called Seder in Hebrew.

[d] The Torah is the first five books of the Jewish Bible, also known as "The Law." Torah is sometimes used in a general sense by Jews when referring to their whole (Old Testament) Bible although "Tanakh" is used the most often. Interestingly, the word "Tanakh" is an acronym composed of the first letters of the three sections of the Hebrew Bible, 1) The Law

fourteenth day of Nisan except for the ritual of smearing of
the blood on the lintel and sideposts which "was never
duplicated again."[26]

When the Jews built the tabernacle and later the
temple, the Passover killing transferred from their homes to
God's appointed center of sacrifice.[e] The head of each family
still killed their own lamb, but it was all done inside the
temple court.[27]

The Jewish historian, Josephus, gives an interesting
insight concerning the immense number of lambs used for
Passover during a first-century celebration. He states, "A
company not less than ten belong to every sacrifice (for it is
unlawful for them to feast singly by themselves), and many
of us are twenty in a company."[28] He calculated that on a
first-century Passover 256,500 lambs were slain!

Twelve Fulfillments

The prophetic significance of this holy day of
Passover is many-fold. I Corinthians 5:7 explains, "*For even
Christ our passover is sacrificed for us.*" Also the Apostle John
pointing to Jesus declares, "*Behold the Lamb of God which taketh
away the sin of the world.*"[f]

Comparing the rituals in Exodus regarding the
Passover lamb to the events which transpired before and
during the Crucifixion of Jesus, brings us to a reverent
conclusion that Jesus is indeed the Lamb of God. Let's look
at twelve of these fulfillments.

(Torah); 2) the Prophets (Neviim); and 3) the Writings (Khetuvim).

[e] Deuteronomy 16: 1-6

[f] John 1:29

1. **Passover and Crucifixion preplanned by God:**
Both the original Passover and its fulfillment in Jesus'
Crucifixion were prophesied by God long before they
occurred.

Words of promise given by God to Abraham include a
prophecy concerning his descendants. God foretold, *"Know
of a surety that thy seed shall be a stranger in a land that is not
theirs, and shall serve them; and they shall afflict them four
hundred years;*

*And also that nation, whom they shall serve, I will judge:
and afterward shall they come out with great substance."*[g]

Just as God foretold, Abraham's descendants all
moved to Egypt upon the invitation of a friendly Pharaoh.
However, after thirty years, the subsequent Pharaohs began
turning against the Jews, eventually forcing them to become
slaves. In time, the Jews cried out to God to deliver them
from bondage. The Lord answered their cry through Moses
whom He had prepared for this task. Exactly 430 years later
(**to the day**), the Passover and ensuing exodus occurred.[h] [29]

The birth and Crucifixion of Jesus was also pre-
planned by God. Scripture tells us that Mary conceived a
child of the Holy Spirit. We also read, *"And she shall bring
forth a son, and thou shalt call his name Jesus: for he shall save his
people from their sins."*[i] In fact seven hundred years earlier
Isaiah prophesied: *"Behold a virgin shall conceive, and bear a son,
and shall call his name Immanuel."*[j]

---

[g] Genesis 15:13,14

[h] Exodus 12:40, 41; Acts 7:6, 7

[i] Matthew 1:21

[j] Isaiah 7:14

Jesus is actually referred to in the Scriptures as *"the lamb slain from the foundation of the world."*[k] (That's certainly preplanning!)

2. Choice of city: The divine plan to provide Jesus as the ultimate Passover lamb is demonstrated in God's choice of Bethlehem as the birth city.

Travelers streaming into Jerusalem for the yearly celebration of Passover needed to purchase lambs for sacrifice. In fact, one particular city had raised lambs for this purpose since Old Testament times. When one visits Israel today, the tour guides often point out this town as "the city where the sacrificial lambs were raised." It is Bethlehem![l] Imagine! Jesus, *"the Lamb of God which taketh away the sin of the world,"* was born in the same city which, for more than one thousand years, had provided sacrificial lambs for Passover.

Notice at the time of Jesus' birth, Old Testament scholars were well aware of the prophecy that Messiah would be born in Bethlehem. The Bible says of Herod, after *"he had gathered all the chief priests and the scribes of the people together, he demanded of them where Christ should be born.*

And they said unto him, In Bethlehem of Judea: for it is written by the prophet,

And thou Bethlehem in the land of Judah, art not the least among the princes of Judah: for out of thee shall come a Governor that shall rule my people Israel."[m]

---

[k] Revelation 13:8

[l] A comparison of Genesis 35:19-21 to Micah 4:8 and 5:2 by David Hocking (Calvary Church, Santa Ana, CA) in his tape series on Genesis demonstrates clearly that Bethlehem was the place where the Jews raised lambs for sacrifice.

[m] Matthew 2:4-6

3. Without blemish: As the Passover lamb must be a male without blemish, so Jesus was a male without blemish. In I Peter 1:18,19 God makes sure we understand that His Son was "*a lamb without blemish and without spot.*" Throughout Jesus' ministry, critics looked for some error, some blemish, to use as a legal reason to reject His claim to be the Son of God, the Messiah.[30] This examination climaxed in an enveloping assault by all of His religious antagonists, to find some error in His life or teaching. This unsuccessful attack began after Jesus' triumphal entry into Jerusalem when He offered Himself to the Jews.[n]

4. Selected on a specific day: Jesus was dedicated as God's sacrificial lamb on the appropriate prophetic day. Just as fifteen hundred years earlier, the Passover lamb was selected on this tenth day of Nisan, so Jesus was set apart for sacrifice on the same date. This can be determined by following the biblical progression of days listed in John 12:1 −12: "*Then Jesus six days before the passover came to Bethany.*"

This passage goes on to tell us that Jesus ate dinner that evening in Bethany, was anointed with oil by Mary, then "*on the next day*" He proceeded through His triumphal entry.

According to the *Jewish Encyclopedia*, counting of days can be inclusive. That is, the count of "one" can begin during a portion of the day on which you begin counting. By simply counting, we can discover that the day which is "*six days before the Passover*" is the ninth day of Nisan. (*See chart on page 47.*)

That means Jesus traveled and arrived in Bethany on the ninth before sundown.[o] As he ate dinner, the evening

[n] Matthew 21:1-9; Mark 11:1-11; Luke 19: 29-38; John 12:12-19

[o] Edersheim in *The Life and Times of Jesus The Messiah* pp. 357, 358 (see bibliography) places the arrival of Jesus on Friday and the supper on Sabbath. (Further discussion of this point will follow.)

HEBREW DAY	GREGORIAN DAY

From sundown to sundown (approx. 6 PM) A day is referred to as "night and day"	From 12 midnight to 12 noon A day is referred to as "day and night"

which began Nisan 10, Mary anointed Jesus with costly perfumed oil. This expensive ointment used primarily for anointing dead bodies because it gave the deceased a sweet smell.[31]

Judas Iscariot immediately criticized this use of oil as an extravagant expenditure of funds. Jesus answered his objection by saying, "*Let her alone; against this day of my burying hath she kept this.*"[p]

The significance of Mary's actions can be discovered in over one hundred references to "anointing" in the Old Testament. A special recipe in Exodus lists the ingredients God wanted in His holy oil. Numerous fragrant spices stirred into olive oil produced the holy oil used for consecrating kings, priests and objects used in service to the Lord.[q] It was also spread on the unleavened bread that was given as an offering to the Lord.[r]

Jesus actually explained that Mary's anointing consecrated Him to God for a sacrificial death.

---

[p] John 12:7

[q] Exodus 29:7, 30:22-33

[r] Exodus 29:2; I Samuel 15:1; Leviticus 8:10

5. **Testing:** The time of Jesus' testing was both the **same length of time** and the **exact dates** that the Passover lambs were originally selected and examined to insure perfection, while staked outside each home to await sacrifice!

"The next day" of John 12:12 is Nisan 11,[s] the triumphal entry of Jesus.[t] This donkey ride into Jerusalem gave a chance for the Jewish nation to receive their Messiah, God's anointed sacrificial lamb. God's offer to the Jews was prophesied in 487 B.C.: *"Rejoice greatly, O daughter of Zion; shout O daughter of Jerusalem: behold thy King cometh unto thee: he is lowly, and riding upon an ass, and upon a colt the foal of an ass."*[u]

As He rode through the streets that day, it appeared that Jesus would be received as the crowds waved palm branches and sang out, *"Hosanna: Blessed is the King of Israel that cometh in the name of the Lord."*[v] How wonderful! The waving of palms along with these words of praise from the Psalms are all part of the Jewish liturgy welcoming the expected Messiah to His Kingdom.[w] Did these celebrants actually recognize Jesus as the Son of God, their Messiah? Unfortunately, as we trace this adoring crowd, a scant three days later, we hear most of these same people shouting, *"Crucify him, crucify him !"*[x]

---

[s] Since the activities of the triumphal entry as well as the traveling Jesus did by coming to Bethany would have broken the Sabbath rules of work and travel, it appears that Jesus had supper Friday evening at Bethany and received local guests only until the Sabbath day was over. This places the triumphal entry on Sunday, Nisan 11.

[t] Many call this day Palm Sunday.

[u] Zechariah 9:9

[v] John 12:13

[w] *See* chapter nine, "Feast of Tabernacles," for more concerning this celebration.

[x] Luke 23:21

Also this "triumphal" day was the beginning of an intense period of testing by the religionists, as related in all four gospels:[y] *"Then went the Pharisees, and took counsel how they might entangle him in his talk."*[z]

After being anointed for burial, the scrutiny by His antagonists lasted four days. Finally, the accusers gave up trying to find fault with Jesus. No error could be found in Him. They instead decided to crucify him with the assistance of false witnesses. These false witnesses couldn't even agree in their lies against Him, and Pilate finally pronounced the actual words, *"I find in him no fault at all."*[aa]

6. **Blood provided life:** Jesus came to die. Just as the blood of the Passover lamb (sprinkled around the doorway) saved the lives of the firstborn children in that house, so the blood of Jesus provides life to those who believe in Him and take shelter in His sacrifice.

God's purpose for blood in sacrifice is explained in Leviticus 17:11, *"For the life of the flesh is in the blood: and I have given it to you upon the altar to make an atonement for your souls: for it is the blood that maketh an atonement for the soul."*

Jesus applied this to himself during the Last Supper as He spoke to His disciples[bb], *"And He took the cup, and gave thanks, and gave it to them, saying, drink ye all of it: For this is my blood of the New Testament, which is shed for many for the remission of sins."*

---

[y] Matthew 22:15-23:39; Mark 12:13-40; Luke 20:1-47; John 12:20-50

[z] Matthew 22:15

[aa] John 18:38

[bb] Matthew 26:27, 28

Finally, to make the blood significance very clear to us, God's Word says[cc], *"How much more shall the blood of Christ, who offered himself without spot to God, purge your conscience from dead works to serve the living God?"*

7. **No bones broken:** Remember, back in Egypt the Jews were expressly instructed not to break any bones of the Passover lamb. The Roman soldiers customarily broke the leg bones of crucified prisoners in order to hasten death. However the Bible **specifically tells us** that the soldiers did not break the legs of Jesus! *"The Jews therefore, because it was the preparation, that the bodies should not remain upon the cross on the sabbath day, (for that sabbath was an high day), besought Pilate that their legs might be broken, and that they might be taken away. But when they came to Jesus, and saw that he was dead already, **they brake not his legs**."*[dd]

8. **Many lambs represented one person:** Based on the number of Jews who left in the Exodus and each household's need for a sacrifice, the first Passover probably required more than 100,000 lambs.[ee] Considering the immense number of lambs sacrificed, take notice of the peculiar way God referred to these lambs in Exodus. God instructed Moses, *"And the whole assembly of the congregation of Israel shall kill it in the evening."*[ff]

God's amazing design is revealed when, despite the existence of thousands of sacrificial lambs, He refers to the sacrifices as a singular "it." This again is a prepicture of

---

[cc] Hebrews 9:14

[dd] John 19:31, 33

[ee] Exodus 12:37

[ff] Exodus 12:6

Jesus, "*the Lamb of God which taketh away the sin of the world.*"[88]
This specific preview of Jesus is mentioned with excitement
by both J. Vernon McGee and Arthur Pink as well as other
noted scholars.[32]

9. **Crucified on Passover Day:** These comparisons
reveal not only that the Passover lamb was a picture of Jesus
Christ, they also show us another amazing parallel. He was
crucified on **the exact day of Passover!** While the Jews were
actually killing the lambs in preparation for the passover
celebration,[33] Jesus was being crucified. Matthew 26:2 states,
"*Ye know that after two days is the feast of the passover, and the
Son of man is betrayed to be crucified.*" John 13:1 tells us, "*Now
before the feast of the passover, when Jesus knew that his hour was
come that he should depart out of this world unto the Father.*"
This is also clearly brought out in John 19:14, 15, "*It was the
preparation of the passover, and about the sixth hour; and he saith
unto the Jews, Behold your King! But they cried out, Away with
him. Pilate saith unto them, Shall I crucify your King? The chief
priests answered, We have no king but Caesar.*"

10. **Hung on the cross as sacrificial lambs brought,
and died at the exact moment sacrificial killing began:**
From instructions in Exodus to "*kill it in the evening,*" we learn
the time that the original Passover lambs were killed. This
term "evening" was an idiom meaning "between evenings"
which referred to the time of 3:00 P.M. until 6:00 P.M.[34] We
also have other information that confirms this time slot for
the slaying of the Passover lambs.

The *Encyclopedia Judaica* states, "It became a general
custom to refrain from labor from 12:00 (noon) onward since
from that time the Paschal sacrifice could properly be
brought."[35]

---

[88] John 1:29

Records also show us that each year at Passover, the priests made sure "the daily burnt offerings were done early, **half past the seventh hour** (1:30 P.M.)[hh] to accommodate Paschal[ii] offerings."[36] According to the *Encyclopedia Judaica*, the last killing at 1:30 P.M. allowed the offering of the daily sacrifice to be completed by 2:30 P.M.[37]

Even writers in Judaism see these events as overlapping. They write, "The Gospel of John...dates the death of Jesus to the 14th of Nisan to the hour of the Passover slaughtering."[38]

According to the records of Josephus, the high priests officiated over the Passover sacrifices from 3:00 P.M. until 5:00 P.M.[39]

When we look yet closer at the events of the Crucifixion day, an astounding probability emerges!

Matthew, Mark, and Luke all refer to a darkness that came over all the earth from 12:00 noon **until 3:00 P.M.**[jj] Since the use of electricity was yet two thousand years away, it seems highly unlikely that the killing of the Passover lambs could have begun until God Himself turned the lights back on **at 3:00 P.M.**!

God gives the exact time of Jesus' death as 3:00 P.M.[kk] It appears that not only was Jesus crucified on Passover, He actually died for us on the cross at 3:00 P.M., the **exact moment** that the slaying of the Passover lambs began!

[hh] Emphasis and Gregorian time is mine.

[ii] Passover.

[jj] Matthew 27:45; Mark 15:33; Luke 23:44, 45

[kk] Matthew 27:46-50; Mark 15:34-37; Luke 23:44-46 (Note in these Scriptures the Jewish time is listed which counted 6:00 a.m. as the first hour.)
How awesome to see also in these references (as well as John 19:30) that even the specific act of dying was done voluntarily by Jesus!

Isn't it overwhelming to see how the seemingly out-of-control mob who crucified Jesus was, in reality, in the hand of God's perfect timing?

11. **Not left on cross overnight:** Remember, the Jews were expressly instructed not to leave any of the sacrificed lamb until the next morning.

God painted another picture of Jesus in His guidelines for Passover. Notice, the Jews insisted that His body not stay on the cross overnight. While it appears the Jews' motives were connected with keeping the letter of the law concerning dead bodies,[ll] they unknowingly fulfilled the rule of **not keeping any of the sacrifice until the next morning.**

12. **Passover night meant death to some and life to others:** Anyone residing in Egypt during Passover night risked the loss of the firstborn child in their home. It didn't matter if they were brave or scared, rich or poor, kind or stingy, religious or atheistic, they all were subject to God's judgment. Only one trait saved their children's lives. That trait was faith—faith that prompted them to follow God's instructions to place the lamb's blood above and beside their doorway.

While the death in each unbelieving home is tragic, the description of the salvation of children in the believing homes is awesome: *"For the Lord will pass through to smite the Egyptians; and when He seeth the blood upon the lintel and upon the two side posts, the Lord will pass over the door, and will not suffer the Destroyer to come in unto your houses to smite you."*[mm]

Arthur Pink gives this heartwarming comment in *Gleanings From Exodus*, "It was not merely that the Lord

---

[ll] Deuteronomy 21:22, 23

[mm] Exodus 12:23

passed by the houses of the Israelites, but that He stood on
guard *protecting* each blood-sprinkled door!"[40]

An Unanswered Question

Jewish scholars have puzzled over the meaning of the
rules attached to this feast. I'd like to quote and then
comment on this astounding statement **from one of their
writers.**

"In particular the Chinuch (no. 7)[nn] suggests that the
emancipation of the Jewish slaves converted them into a
'priestly kingdom.' The "pesach"[oo] was therefore served as a
royal feast, and it was to be eaten in the manner of royalty.
Consequently, the meat was to be well roasted, a process
preferred by royalty because the taste of the meat is brought
out to best advantage. Similarly, no bones were to be broken
because royalty discards the bones whole, but the poor break
the bones so that they can pick them bare of their meat. This
homiletic interpretation is not consistent with the provision
for the eating of the lamb with matza and bitter herbs, in
commemoration of affliction and bitterness. **One could
hardly commemorate royalty and poverty at the same
time.**"[41pp]

In short, this Jewish theologian is puzzling over the
presence of both royalty and affliction in the typology of the
Passover meal. He believes the remembrance of royalty and
the remembrance of poverty at the same time is
incompatible.

This portion of the Passover table has indeed been a
stumbling block to the Jews, as predicted by **their own King**

[nn] Jewish commentary

[oo] Passover.

[pp] Emphasis mine.

David. David writes, "*Let their table become a snare before them: and that which should have been for their welfare, let it become a trap.*"[99]

Christians see no conflict in one feast that celebrates both affliction and royalty. This portion of the feast is seen as a God-designed picture of Jesus Christ as the suffering Savior and the future reigning King.

After the time of King David, upon finishing the Passover meal, those gathered around the Passover table sang the Hallel (Psalms 113–118).[rr] Woven into these psalms is another solemn warning from God. He speaks, even in the songs sung at Passover, concerning the expected refusal of the Jews to recognize the Savior Jesus, the Lamb of the Passover: "*The stone which the builder refused is become the headstone of the corner.*"[ss] We know this is a reference to Jesus from the Scripture. "*Behold, I lay in Sion a chief corner stone, elect, precious: and he that believeth on him shall not be confounded.*

Unto you therefore which believe he is precious: but unto them which be disobedient, the stone which the builders disallowed, the same is made the head of the corner.

And a stone of stumbling, and a rock of offence, even to them which stumble at the word, being disobedient: whereunto also they were appointed."[tt]

Let us who claim the name of Christ, beware lest we also disregard the deep, personal significance represented in Passover. For our sakes Jesus "*became poor,*" that through His

---

[99] Psalm 69:22

[rr] This is the hymn referred to in Mark 14:22-26.

[ss] Psalm 118:22

[tt] I Peter 2:6-8

poverty we might be rich,"[uu] was *"afflicted for our sin,"*[vv] and is also our *"King of Kings."*[ww] Yes, we know that as King, He will reign on earth during the future Millennium, but He should also be reigning in our hearts today.[xx] As Jesus enjoined, *"Why call ye me, Lord, Lord, and do not the things I say?"*[yy]

REVIEW OF FEAST OF PASSOVER (PESACH)

Almost fifteen hundred years before Christ, God called Moses to lead the Jewish nation out of bondage in Egypt. Their release came after the firstborn child in every house of Egypt died at the hand of the Lord. Miraculously, the firstborn in each Jewish family lived because of the lamb's blood they placed around the doorway. The yearly Passover meal is a memorial of those saved lives and the nation's release from slavery.

God's prophetic picture in Passover is His Lamb. Jesus Christ provided salvation and release from bondage for all who trust in the power of His blood and, by faith, place it over the door of their own life.

The **precise** description and instructions of Passover are graphically demonstrated in the Crucifixion of Jesus Christ:

1) Jesus came as foretold. Passover also occurred as foretold!

[uu] II Corinthians 8:9

[vv] Isaiah 53:5-7; I Peter 2:23, 24

[ww] I Timothy 6:14, 15

[xx] Revelation 19:16, 20:6; Romans 10:9

[yy] Luke 6:46

2) Jesus was born in the city where the Passover lambs were raised!

3) Jesus was a male without blemish just as the lambs were!

4) Jesus was chosen for sacrificial death on the same date that Passover lambs were selected!

5) Jesus was tested for perfection for the same length of time and on the exact dates the Passover lambs were observed!

6) Jesus provided salvation through His blood just as the blood of the Passover lambs provided life!

7) Jesus had no bones broken and neither did the lambs!

8) Jesus was the "one" referred to by God as "it" even though the number of lambs slain was plural!

9) Jesus was crucified on the exact day of Passover!

10) Jesus was crucified not only at the same general time of day as the Passover lambs, apparently He died at the exact moment the first group of Passover lambs were slain!

11) Jesus' body did not remain on the cross overnight just as none of the lamb could remain until morning!

12) Jesus provides life to those who trust Him as God's sacrifice just as life came to Jews who believed God

and stayed in the houses marked by the lamb's blood!

CHAPTER 4
UNLEAVENED BREAD (Feast #2)

SPRING	
NISAN 14	NISAN 15
Preparation for Passover	Unleavened Dinner

This celebration began on the Passover preparation day of Nisan 14 by the removal of all leaven from the houses. Celebrants ate the feast of Passover and unleavened bread after sundown (which made it the fifteenth of the month). The festival continued for seven days and no work could be done on the first or the last day of the seven. Since Jews scrupulously eliminated all leaven from their homes, the only bread eaten during this protracted feast was flat, unleavened bread. The observance of this holy convocation commemorated the hurried release of the Jews from the bondage of Egypt (Exodus 12:14−20; Leviticus 23:6−8).

The Meaning of Leaven

The presence of leaven (yeast) in bread causes it to rise and become fluffy and full. Bread baked without leaven is plain and flat but does not spoil. However, since leaven is actually a live fungus, bread baked with it will mold and become inedible.

We are taught in the Bible that leaven is a picture of sin and false religion. Sin, like leaven, may appear attractive but it causes decay. Note Jesus' statements, "*Take heed and beware of the leaven of the Pharisees and Sadducees,*"[a] and "*Beware ye of the leaven of the Pharisees, which is hypocrisy.*"[b] God cautions us, "*Your glorying is not good. Know ye not that a little leaven leaveneth the whole lump? Purge out therefore the old leaven, that ye may be a new lump, as ye are unleavened. For even Christ our passover is sacrificed for us: Therefore let us keep the feast not with the old leaven of malice and wickedness; but with the unleavened bread of sincerity and truth.*"[c]

What a beautiful picture! Jesus, through his sacrifice, purged sin from mankind. The Bible says, "*How much more shall the blood of Christ, who through the eternal Spirit offered himself without spot to God, purge with blood?*" and "*without the shedding of blood there is no remission.*"[d]

Also in this feast Jesus is prepictured in the unleavened bread itself. Mary's act of anointing Jesus, four days before His Crucifixion, reminds us of the spreading of oil on the unleavened bread used for sacrifice.[e] Only Jesus could be represented by unleavened bread because only He lived a sinless life.

How amazing! After Jesus was crucified, the Jews were celebrating The Feast of Unleavened Bread while Jesus was actually purging sin (leaven) for us!

---

[a] Matthew 16:6

[b] Luke 12:1

[c] I Corinthians 5:6-8

[d] Hebrews 9: 14, 22

[e] Numbers 6:15; John 12:1-8

REVIEW OF FEAST OF UNLEAVENED BREAD
(HAG-HA MATZOT)

During Passover, the Jews began a week-long celebration which commemorated their hasty departure from Egypt. The only bread eaten during this feast week is unleavened.

Leaven in the Bible is a symbol of sin. This taking away of leaven is a graphic picture of Jesus taking away our sin. He actually took the punishment for everyone's sin.

CHAPTER 5
FIRSTFRUITS (Feast #3)

SPRING		
NISAN 14	NISAN 15	SUN. AFTER SABBATH
Preparation for Passover	Unleavened Dinner	Firstfruits, Resurrection

God instructed Moses in Leviticus 23:10, 11, "*When ye come into the land which I give unto you, and shall reap the harvest thereof, then ye shall bring a sheaf of the firstfruits of your harvest unto the priest: And he shall wave the sheaf before the Lord, to be accepted for you: on the morrow after the sabbath the priest shall wave it.*"

The Jews were to begin celebration of this feast when they arrived in the Promised Land. Leviticus, chapter 23 shows that God gave this ordinance to the Jews so they would remember the first harvest that He would provide for them in the land of Israel.

Israel was instructed to have the High Priest bring one sheaf of the firstfruits of the harvest (which represented the whole harvest), and wave it before the Lord. This spring festival became the first harvest celebration of each year.

There is a difference of opinion among theologians, both Jewish and Christian, as to when this feast is to be celebrated. We will take time to examine both viewpoints because of the prophetic application of Firstfruits. A few days difference may seem inconsequential to us, but when

God is painting a picture of His beloved Son Jesus Christ, every stroke of His brush is purposeful.

The extreme importance of determining the exact day God intended for the celebration of Firstfruits has to do with the character of God. If He cannot lie, if He is all-knowing, and if nothing is too hard for Him, then the prophetic pictures He paints throughout the Bible must be fulfilled in exact detail!

For instance, if God's Old Testament pictures of Jesus showed us that Jesus would literally be in the grave three days and three nights, then resurrection short of this time period would indicate a lack of knowledge and control on the part of God. As we examine the prophetic pictures of the exact day of both the Crucifixion and the Resurrection, bear in mind the reason for this detailed inspection. God is sovereign! His absolute control over the affairs of man is graphically demonstrated through the timing of the Crucifixion, death, burial, and Resurrection of His beloved son Jesus Christ.

Different Ideas on Firstfruits

Some commentators have postulated that the Sabbath referred to in Leviticus 23:11 is the Sabbath (Feast) of Unleavened Bread. They conclude that Firstfruits is always to be observed on Nisan 16. It is said by some that a statement of Josephus "proves beyond a doubt" that the Jews celebrated Firstfruits on Nisan 16.[42]

There are several problems with this position. First, it's somewhat precarious to come to a "positive" biblical conclusion based solely on the words of a historian. Although historical writings are useful in understanding the holy Scriptures, man's words cannot be deemed "inspired."

Historically speaking the question as to which day or date was the correct one to celebrate Firstfruits has been debated by the Jews themselves. The Pharisees interpreted the Sabbath in Leviticus 23:10 – 16 to be the Sabbath Feast of Unleavened Bread. This resulted in their celebrating Nisan 16 as Firstfruits which indeed became the predominant view.

We cannot, however, fail to notice that the Sadducees firmly held to their belief that the Sabbath referred to in Leviticus 23 was the seventh-day Sabbath. This system produces a different date each year for the celebration of Firstfruits.

The Qumran community had yet another idea for the celebration of Firstfruits. They used a fixed solar calendar and maintained that the Sabbath at the end of the Passover festival was the one referred to in Leviticus. From this interpretation, Nisan 26 was always celebrated as Firstfruits.[43]

Since the Jews themselves did not agree on the time for Firstfruits and since Jesus made no comment in the Gospels about the feast, we must look beyond tradition to find a solid answer.

With regard to Firstfruits in particular, the scriptural context helps us to determine an understanding of which Sabbath is involved. We can see in Leviticus 23, that five of the seven feasts have definite months and days on which they are to be celebrated.

Note that **no specific date** (i.e., month and day) is given for the Feast of Firstfruits or the Feast of Weeks. Both of these festivals are said to **follow a particular day of the week** by a set number of days. This leads us to see that the day of the month on which they both would fall is variable. They do, however, occur each year on the same day of the week.

This leads us to prefer the selection of Firstfruits as **the Sunday after the Sabbath following Passover.**[*] This

---

[*] Danny Litvin in "Pentecost Is Jewish" pp. 3, 9 and Appendix I (see Bibliography) also concurs with this conclusion in his work on this subject.

interpretation seems more likely, since God left the notable absence of a specific date for this feast.

What Firstfruits Means

The picture presented to us in Firstfruits as New Testament Christians is awe-inspiring! *"But now is Christ risen from the dead, and become the firstfruits of them that slept."*[b] Jesus is the firstfruits from the dead!

Another aspect of this feast can be discovered by reviewing two important pieces of information. From these we will see the careful planning and absolute control of God with regard to Firstfruits and **the year** in which Jesus was crucified.

1. Jesus said He would be at least three days and three nights in the heart of the earth but no longer than three.[c]

2. Easter, when we celebrate **the discovery of the Resurrection** of Jesus, is on Sunday. This allows the three days and three nights to fall between the Crucifixion and Sunday.

According to the original Jewish calendar, every year there would be a different length of time between Passover and Firstfruits. **The year Jesus was crucified,** Passover preceded Sunday by the exact number of days needed to allow **three days** to fit in between. Jesus was crucified on Nisan 14. He conquered death after three days and nights (Nisan 17) so that Sunday the Festival of Firstfruits, on Nisan 18, would be our day to celebrate His Resurrection.

---

[b] I Corinthians 15:20

[c] Matthew 27:62-64

Again, God is altogether true to His Old Testament pictures. As the Jews were following the rituals of Firstfruits, the disciples celebrated the Resurrection of Jesus **in the presence of Jesus,** the firstfruits from the dead!

Prepictured Timing of the Resurrection

The Jews left Egypt on Nisan 15.[d] Through Moses, the Jews had only requested permission to take a three-day journey into the desert to worship the Lord. The Bible states they camped on the shores of the Red Sea which would be the third day or Nisan 17.

Pharaoh once again changed his mind about letting the Jews go to worship the Lord. He mustered his army and galloped into the desert to bring back his Jewish slaves. God surprised everyone by miraculously dividing the waters of the Red sea, providing a way of escape for the Jews. Pharaoh and his army saw this avenue of escape but when they tried to follow the path prepared through the sea, the water closed over them, drowning everyone.[e]

The count of days involved here has startling significance. Three days from the first Passover, the Jews were delivered from death unto life! The day of Nisan 18 brought jubilation to the rescued Jews. God literally brought them from death unto life.

On that day (Nisan 18) the newly rescued Jews sang, *"Thou in thy mercy hast led forth the people which thou hast redeemed; thou hast guided them in thy strength unto thy holy habitation"*[f] in celebration of their new life. Just so believers in Jesus Christ now sing, "Because He lives, I can face

---

[d] Exodus 12:30, 31

[e] Exodus 14

[f] Exodus 15:13

tomorrow!" The celebration words of the New Testament quoted from the Old Testament prophet Hosea[g] say, *"O death, where is thy sting? O grave where is thy victory?"*[h]

The amazing rescue of the Jews from the tyrant of Egypt paints a prophetic picture of God's preplanned rescue of all mankind from the ownership of Satan. The Bible says, *"For to this end Christ both died, and rose, and revived, that he might be the Lord of both the dead and the living."*[i] God provided an avenue of life through the Red Sea for the believing Jews yet this same avenue became a place of judgment for the God-rejecting Egyptians!

This path of either rescue or judgment is still an option to mankind today. The Bible says, *"For God sent not his son into the world to condemn the world; but that the world through him might be saved. He that believeth on him is not condemned: but he that believeth not is condemned already, because he hath not believed in the name of the only begotten Son of God."*[j]

Notice the length of time from the slaying of the Passover lamb (Nisan 14) to the rescue from Egypt and the tyranny of Pharaoh (Nisan 17) and also to the next-day celebration of their completed redemption (Nisan 18).

Now, compare these events and their timing to the Crucifixion of Jesus. We see Jesus' death, His three days in the grave, followed by the joyous Easter celebration of His Resurrection.

---

[g] Hosea 13:14

[h] I Corinthians 15:55

[i] Romans 14:9

[j] John 3:17-18

Other Pictures

Just to make sure we understand the significance of Nisan 17, God gave even more prepictures of this vital day of rescue from death.

Scripture tells us that Noah's Ark containing the only survivors of the universal judgment flood, touched solid ground on **Nisan 17**.[k]

Again in Esther we see the entire nation of Jews being snatched from certain annihilation on God's special day of **Nisan 17!**[l]

REVIEW OF FEAST OF FIRSTFRUITS (BIKKURIM)

As thanks for the first harvest in their Promised Land, the Jews offered a sheaf of grain to the Lord. This special day came every year on the Sunday that followed the Saturday after Passover.

The first person ever to rise from the dead, never to die again, is Jesus Christ. Joyful Christians celebrate this harvest of Resurrection every year on Easter Sunday. The Bible actually calls Jesus "the Firstfruits from the dead."

---

[k] Genesis 8:4. Mankind followed God's original civil calendar at this time which made Nisan the seventh month.

[l] A careful reading of Esther 3-7 especially 3:7, 12, 4:16, 5:1, 14, 6:1, 14 and 7:1, 2, 10 show Nisan 17 as the day of national rescue.

CHAPTER 6
FEAST OF WEEKS (Feast #4)

SPRING			
NISAN 14	NISAN 15	SUN. AFTER SABBATH	50 DAYS LATER
Preparation for Passover	Unleavened Dinner	Firstfruits, Resurrection	Weeks, Pentecost

Fifty days after Firstfruits, the Jews offered two loaves of bread, baked with leaven, as a second offering to the Lord: *"Ye shall count unto you from the morrow after the sabbath from the day that ye brought the sheaf of the wave offerings[Feast of Firstfruits]: seven sabbaths shall be complete: Even unto the morrow after the seventh sabbath shall ye number fifty days...Ye shall bring out of your habitation two wave-loaves...of fine flour...baken with leaven"* (Leviticus 23:15–17). This comprised a second harvest festival, but notice the use of leaven this time.

This information becomes particularly exciting to Christians when we recognize that the fifty-day celebration of the Feast of Weeks was known in the days of the New Testament as **Pentecost**. This name, Pentecost (which Christians revere because it was the day the Holy Spirit descended on believers), is derived from the Greek for **fiftieth**. Imagine, just as the Jews were offering the two loaves of bread to the Lord, God sent His Holy Spirit to live inside of His believers!

As Christians, the significance of this feast is best savored by reading John 14:25, 26 and Acts 2:1–47. In these verses Jesus promised that when He went back to heaven, He would send the Holy Spirit to all believers to empower and to guide them. The day of Pentecost is considered the birth of the New Testament Church.[a] Jesus said, "*But ye shall receive power, after that the Holy Ghost is come upon you: and ye shall be witnesses unto me both in Jerusalem, and in Judea, and in Samaria, and unto the uttermost part of the earth.*"[b]

For the first time, both Jews and Gentiles would carry the Gospel message from God. Later God mentions these two groups, but says He is God of both of them.[c]

What a thrill to fathom the deep symbolism of the Feast of Weeks. The two loaves offered to the Lord represent the birth of the New Testament Church comprised of both Jews and Gentiles.[d]

This prophetic meaning is taught by Victor Buksbazen in *The Feasts of Israel* who adds, "The three thousand Jewish believers were the spiritual firstfruits of the church of Christ. Thus the Old Testament symbol, the two wave-loaves, became a glorious reality in the New—**a church composed of Jewish and Gentile believers**, purchased by the blood of the Lamb."[44]

---

[a] The "Church" means "the called out ones."

[b] Acts 1:8

[c] Romans 3:29

[d] The command for two loaves to represent the Church rather than a single loaf strengthens the promises of God to the nation of Israel. Although the Church is Jew and Gentile combined into a single group, God still remembers His chosen people. Romans, chapter 11 teaches that Israel is the olive tree and the Gentiles are grafted-in branches. One day this special time of the "Church" on earth will be over and the spotlight of God will once again be shining upon the olive tree (Jewish nation).

Could God's inclusion of leaven in this bread be representative of seeing this new group as including some error?

The bread of the Passover contained no leaven because it is a picture of perfect Jesus whose body was broken for us.[e] The leavened bread, however, may picture the Church which is not without error, even though we are forgiven. Note, *"Who shall change our vile bodies?"*[f] as well as Paul's accurate description of our remaining weakness to sin, *"For the good that I would I do not; but the evil which I would not that I do. Now if I do that I would not, it is no more I that do it, but sin that dwelleth in me."*[g] Scofield notes state, "Leaven is present, because there is evil in the church."[h45]

Once again, a beautiful prophetic picture of God unfurls:

- The Feast of Weeks and the day of Pentecost occur fifty days after Firstfruits.

- The two loaves combined into one offering reminds us of Jews and Gentiles both being included in the New Testament Church.

- The leaven in the loaves reminds us that the members of the Church are not without sin.

---

[e] I Corinthians 11:24

[f] Philippians 3;20, 21

[g] Romans 7:19, 20

[h] Matthew 13:13; Acts 5:1,10; 15:1

An Interesting Probability

To Jewish writers, the giving of the Law on Mount Sinai is known as "the espousal of Israel to God."[i]

Note the scriptural tie-in of the wilderness journey to espousal. *"Go and cry in the ears of Jerusalem, saying Thus saith the Lord; I remember thee, the kindness of thy youth, the love of thine espousals, when thou wentest after me in the wilderness, in a land that was not sown. Israel was holiness unto the Lord, and the firstfruits of his increase."[j]*

According to Jewish historians, "A new theme was added to the festival of Shavuot after the destruction of the temple in A.D. 70."[46]   The rabbis began to teach that Moses received the Law on Mount Sinai exactly fifty days after the Jews crossed the Red Sea (following their exit from Egypt).

Actually, the exact time of the giving of the Law, to the day, is hard to prove conclusively from the Bible. However, Scripture does give us excellent indications of the time gap between the Exodus and the giving of the Law.

As previously shown, the Jews killed the Passover lamb on Nisan 14, left Egypt on Nisan 15, passed through the Red Sea on Nisan 17 and celebrated their redemption on the Nisan 18. We can count from the day the Jews celebrated their new life of freedom until the day indicated in the Bible that they reached the area of Mount Sinai to calculate the days that had transpired.

Scripture states, *"In the third month, when the children of Israel were gone forth out of the land of Egypt, the same day they*

---

[i] Jewish belief is that, "God as the bride's father gives as dowry the 613 commandments, the Bible, Talmud and other sacred writings. Moses presents as dowry to his son — the people of Israel — the prayer shawl and phylacteries, the Sabbath and festivals. The contracts are witnessed by God and his servant Moses" (Najara Israel in *The Shavuot Anthology* by Philip Goodman).

[j] Jeremiah 2:2, 3

came into the wilderness of Sinai."[k] In the Hebrew text the word translated "same" gives the indication that it was the third day as well as the third month. The number of days from the first month[l] (Nisan 18—their rescue from bondage in Egypt) to the third day of the third month (their arrival in the wilderness of Sinai) would be forty-six days.

The Lord then told Moses to prepare for the third day on which God Himself will come down in the sight of the people on Mount Sinai. Moses went up the mountain and received laws for the Jews to live by as well as a verbal list of the Ten Commandments.

This sequence of events reasonably places the giving of the Law to the children of Israel on the fiftieth day after their rescue from Egypt. (The Feast of Weeks—also known as Shavuot or Pentecost—is celebrated, as mentioned, on the fiftieth day after Firstfruits.)

Interestingly, extra-biblical sources (besides rabbis) such as Falashas[m] and the book of Jubilees[n] also state that the Law was given on Shavuot (Feast of Weeks).[47]

Although it's hard to know conclusively from the Scriptures listed in this study that the Law was given on Mount Sinai on the fifty-day Feast of Weeks, the parallel meanings of the events are amazing! An in-depth comparison of these two occurrences is done by Danny Litvin in *Pentecost Is Jewish.*[48]

By comparing Exodus 19:16 – 19 to Acts 2:2 – 15, Litvin points out the similarities between the giving of the Law and Pentecost. "The parallels are many: the time of day, the type of sound that was heard, the reaction of the people,

---

[k] Exodus 19:1

[l] Exodus 12:1

[m] Jews of Ethiopia.

[n] Second century B.C.

the fire representing God, and the location—the central point for the Jewish people."

He goes on to show that the purposes of both the Law and the Holy Spirit were the same. They both give direction to mankind as to how to live life in the way God requires, convict mankind of sin and guilt, keep the believers separated from the world, mark those who belong to God, and point to God the Father.[49]

Because of the intricate skill God uses in weaving messages into the fabric of His word, this premise is probably true.

However, the wondrous truth we do know is that **the Jewish Feast of Weeks is Pentecost, the birth of the Church!**

REVIEW OF FEAST OF WEEKS (SHAVUOT)

Seven weeks and one day (fifty days) after the harvest celebration of Firstfruits, the Jews celebrated Feast of Weeks. Part of this feast involved offering the Lord two loaves of bread, baked with leaven. This commemorated a second harvest and again the Jews thanked God for His provisions.

Forty days after Jesus Christ's Resurrection, He ascended into Heaven. Ten days after this ascension, just as the Jews were celebrating Pentecost (Feast of Weeks), God fulfilled a promise made by Jesus. On this very day the new believers gathered in Jerusalem, received the indwelling of the promised Holy Spirit.

This extraordinary event marks the birth of the Church. God tells us that the Church is made up of both Jews and Gentiles. Although Jesus can be represented by unleavened bread, mankind cannot. The two loaves with leaven represent Jews and Gentiles alongside each other as a worship offering to the Lord.

✡ ✡ ✡ ✡ ✡ ✡

SECTION III
FEAST DAYS YET UNFULFILLED

Interestingly, the four preceding Jewish spring feasts prepicture events connected with the first coming of Jesus.

After the fourth feast, which is a harvest festival, a notable time gap of nearly four months elapses before the remaining three feasts transpire in the autumn. The first of these fall celebrations is yet another harvest festival.

God describes these two harvest times as the "former" and the "latter" rain. How significant that God also uses these two times of rain to depict the first and Second Coming of Jesus![50]

Jesus makes reference to this gap between harvests after His encounter with the Samaritan woman. In speaking to His disciples concerning the importance of going to everyone with the gospel he warns, *"Say not ye, There are yet four months, and then cometh harvest? Behold, I say unto you, lift up your eyes, and look on the fields; for they are white already to harvest"*(John 4:35).

Was Jesus using this four month gap as a picture of the believer's responsibility during the Church age (the time between His first and Second Coming) to *"Go ye therefore, and teach all nations"*as recorded in Matthew 28:19?

Could this gap also be the two days[a] mentioned in Hosea after which God will revive the nation of Israel? Hosea describes God punishing the Jews for a time which lasts until *"they acknowledge their offence, and seek my face."*[b] Are we to look for two twenty-four hour days to fulfill this prophecy of judgment or possibly two thousand years? Since the use of a number (two) shows us that a specific period of time is given, and since historically the Jews did not return to the Lord in two twenty-four hour days, perhaps the length of time intended in Hosea is two thousand years (garnered from the Scripture *"a thousand years as one day"*).[c]

The remaining three feasts fall in the month of Tishri. To the Jews the fifth feast, Rosh HaShanah, is the day of judgment; the sixth feast, Yom Kippur, is the day of atonement; and the seventh, Succoth, is the season of rejoicing. These three feasts have yet to see their New Testament fulfillment.

God was exact to the day in timing the events that the first four feasts represented:

- Passover depicted Christ's Crucifixion.

- Unleavened Bread pictured the purging of sin.

- Firstfruits foretold Jesus' Resurrection.

---

[a] The Hebrew word for day, "yowm" has a variety of definitions. It not only can be referring to a twenty-four hour day, it can also denote part of a day, an age, a required season, or many other meanings. As with many other Hebrew words, the context determines its exact meaning.

[b] Hosea 5:15-6:2

[c] Psalm 90:4; II Peter 3:8

• Weeks illustrated the birth of the Church.

Could we then expect the last three feasts not only to be pictures of coming events, but also to occur on the same day of the year as their ancient counterparts? Do these three last feasts represent the time Jesus calls His bride,[d51] returns to the earth a second time, and sets up His earthly kingdom?

---

d Some expositors feel that no event relating to the Church can be found in the Old Testament because the Church is "a mystery yet unrevealed." *See* endnote for further discussion.

CHAPTER 7
FEAST OF THE TRUMPETS (Feast #5)

SPRING				FALL
NISAN 14	NISAN 15	SUN. AFTER SABBATH	50 DAYS LATER	TISHRI 1
Preparation for Passover	Unleavened Dinner	Firstfruits, Resurrection	Weeks, Pentecost	Trumpets, Rapture

Today, this feast is called Rosh HaShanah by the Jews. It occurs almost four months after the Feast of Weeks, falling in September or October. God instructed them to celebrate a sabbath by a blowing of trumpets.

Leviticus 23:24 says "*In the Seventh month, in the first day of the month shall ye have a sabbath, a memorial of blowing of trumpets, an holy convocation.*" Although no more details are given in the Bible as to how to execute this blowing, it's fascinating to study the way the Jews traditionally observe this day.

According to the Talmud (Jewish comments on the legal sections of the Torah), the Jews attached an additional day of observance to this feast. This apparently occurred around 500 B.C., about one thousand years after the guidelines in Leviticus were given.[52] Historically, this change came about because of the Rabbis' desire to make sure all the people realized the new moon had been spied so that Rosh HaShanah could be declared. Since this feast inaugurated the new year, they felt the necessity of a two-day celebration. Authentication of each month's beginning was determined by reports of witnesses who testified to seeing the new moon. In order to avoid the error of celebrating the feast one day early or of missing by one day, thus causing the whole year's calendar to be askew, they added an extra day. This decision also resulted from an expressed concern that Jews living in outlying districts might not hear the proclamation in time to celebrate.[53]

They began the celebration of this feast during the previous month by blowing a ram's horn trumpet for twenty-nine days. On the last day of the month the blowing stopped. Then on the first day of Tishri (Rosh HaShanah), one more blowing of the trumpet occurred. This blowing consisted of three distinct series (of thirty blasts each) which then concluded with a blowing of ten blasts. At the end of all these blowings, there was one last, long sounding of the trumpet. It was called "Teki'ah Gedolah" which means, "The Great Blowing."[54]

Trumpet blowing is mentioned more than fifty times in the Old Testament. Although this sound was used to lead the people and to precede announcements, "gathering the people" describes the main use of the shofar,[a] or trumpet blast.[b]

Although each of the seven months, Nisan through Tishri, was introduced on its first day by the blowing of a trumpet, this fifth feast became known as the "Day of Blowing" or "Yom Teruah" by the Jews. Selection of this name came from Numbers 29:1 which refers to this feast day as "a day of blowing the trumpets." Since Tishri, the month of this Feast, had become the first month on the Jewish civil calendar, the Jews later began to call this feast day "Rosh HaShanah" which means "the beginning of the year."

---

[a] Usually made from a ram's horn. Other trumpets were crafted from silver.

[b] Exodus 19:13-19; Joshua 6:1-16

Amazing Information

An amazing fact emerges in the writings of Jewish theologians concerning Rosh HaShanah. They inform us that the shofar's message "was interpreted also as a symbol of the **last trump** and as the rallying call of Israel in it's eternal battle for the Kingdom of God."[55] Interestingly this is not literally the last trumpet to be blown in the festivals of the Jews. There are more blowings yet to come, including a particularly important one on Yom Kippur.

This amazing symbolic reference to the "last trump" contains profound implications for the Christian student of prophecy! After we finish unfolding the Jewish view of this feast day, we will compare this special name for Rosh HaShanah to the New Testament Scriptures.

Several possible reasons arise as to why this festival day became known by the people as the "last trump" day. First of all this festival day which featured one hundred blasts of the trumpet,[56] was the last festival month on the calendar given to the Jews in Leviticus.[57] Secondly, this day closed with a single long blast of the shofar that became louder and louder until it ended.[58] This long blast reminded the Jews of the sustained trumpet blast that increased in loudness when the Lord came down to Mount Sinai to speak to Moses.[c]

Joseph Good of Hatikva Ministries[d] gives an excellent presentation on this aspect of Rosh HaShanah. He explains that the "last trump" idiom for this feast comes from the Jewish connection of the ram's horn (shofar) with the ram that replaced Isaac as a sacrifice.[e59] He explains that the Jews

---

[c] Exodus 19:19

[d] A comprehensive teacher of Jewish Festivals from a Christian perspective.

[e] Genesis 22:1-14

believed that the ram caught in the thicket represented Messiah. They also teach that the left horn of this ram became the shofar blown on Mount Sinai at the giving of the Law. This blowing of the ram's horn became known as the "first trump."

Later in the festival of Rosh HaShanah, the Jews again make a connection with the ram substituted for Isaac. Regarding this association, Abraham Bloch, highly acclaimed Jewish author, records "The offspring of Isaac will someday transgress my will, and I will judge them on Rosh HaShanah. Should they appeal to my leniency, I will recall the binding of Isaac and let them blow then the horn of this ram [which was substituted for Isaac]."† [60]

Joseph Good, in his tape series, states that the shofar blown on Rosh HaShanah is considered to be the right horn of the ram in the binding of Isaac. Because of this connection with the remaining horn of the ram, this festival day acquired the additional name of, the "last trump" day.[61]

The Jewish belief about Rosh HaShanah is that it is:

1. A day of judgment, a call for repentance, and a time of regathering for the nation. Jewish writers tell us, "Isaiah explicitly associated the sound of the shofar with an admonition against sin. *'Cry aloud, spare not, lift up your voice like a shofar, and declare unto my people their transgression, and to the house of Jacob their sin.'*(Isaiah 58:1) **The ingathering of the Jewish people and its ultimate return to God will be announced by a prolonged blast of the shofar.**§ *'And it will come to pass in that day that a great shofar shall be blown, and they shall come that were lost in the land of Assyria, and they that were*

---

† Abraham P. Bloch, *The Biblical and Historical Background of the Jewish Holy Days* p. 25 (KTAV Publishing House, INC New NY 1978).

§ Emphasis mine.

dispersed in the land of Egypt, and they shall worship the Lord in the holy mountain in Jerusalem'(Isaiah 27:13)."[62]

2. A day of judgment for **all people.**[h]   "Man is judged on Rosh HaShanah, and the verdict is sealed on Yom Kippur."[63] The Talmud states, "At the new year all creatures pass before him like sheep, as it is stated: He that fashions the heart of them all, that considers all their doings."[64]

3. A day "to confound and to confuse Satan, who, the Rabbis thought had a special predilection of accusing Israel on New Year's day, bringing up before the Lord all their shortcomings and sins."[65]

An Exciting Picture

When one looks at the verses that describe the Rapture, there is a fascinating similarity to the Feast of the Trumpets. In I Thessalonians 4:16−18, we are taught that Jesus will come for the believers, *"with the trump of God."* More specifically, Paul wrote concerning the Rapture in I Corinthians 15:51, 52, *"Behold, I show you a mystery; We shall not all sleep, but we shall all be changed, In a moment in the twinkling of an eye, <u>at the last trump</u>: for the trumpet shall sound, and the dead in Christ shall be raised incorruptible, and we shall be changed."*

For nearly two thousand years the believers in Christ have quoted these words of promise with excitement. How strange that we could so lovingly cherish each word of this special promise yet never once ask ourselves why Paul referred to the trumpet blast as "the last trump." We know that literally this is not the last trumpet to blow in the

---

[h] Emphasis mine.

revealed plan of God.[i] In fact there are many more trumpet sounds yet to follow as recorded for us in the book of Revelation.

Could it be that the Hebrew believers of the first-century quite easily understood this "last trump" reference to be Rosh HaShanah because they understood the Jewish festivals and the different names by which they were known? This may be an example of how the lack of in-depth study of the Jewish holy days has caused many Christians throughout the centuries to miss important prophetic information in the Bible.

Since the Rapture is a gathering of believers and since the trumpet in the Old Testament was used primarily for gathering the people, let's consider the possibility that Rosh HaShanah may actually be the **day of the year** that the Rapture occurs.

The Great Gathering

Following the escape from Egypt and the return to the Promised Land, Jews have looked back to their rescue in celebration and praise. But God prophesies a rescue coming yet in the future that will completely overshadow this remembrance: "*Therefore, behold, the days come, saith the LORD, that it shall no more be said, The LORD liveth, that brought up the children of Israel out of the land of Egypt; But, The LORD liveth, that brought up the children of Israel from the land of the north, and from all the lands whither he had driven them:*

---

[i] Some have taken this "last trump" blowing to be the last of the seven trumpet blasts in Revelation, chapter 11. However, since the use of trumpet blasts is essentially Jewish, it is necessary to interpret their meaning in light of Jewish understanding.

According to all Jewish theology the "Last Trumpet" blast during Rosh HaShanah is by no means the last use of trumpets during the seven festivals. The holy day of Yom Kippur ends with a blowing called the "Great Trumpet blast" (as outlined in the chapter on Yom Kippur).

and I will bring them again into their land that I gave unto their fathers."ʲ

In the early 1900's, a number of Christian scholars suggested that the Trumpet Feast was the call for Israel to regather.[66] However, today most scholars agree that although it is obvious that God assisted the Jews in regaining ownership of Israel, we have not yet seen the true "regathering." To understand their reasoning one only needs to observe that even though the Jews once again possess their homeland, only six million of the world's (at least) thirteen million Jews live in Israel.ᵏ

Devotees of Bible prophecy were correct to thrill in 1948 when the land of Israel gained international recognition as the homeland of the Jews. However, this return is more of a restoration of the land than a fulfillment of the prophesied "regathering."ˡ This restoration needed to transpire in order to 1) prepare the land to be occupied by a huge nation of people by the end of the seven-year Tribulation and 2) set in power a Jewish state with whom the Antichrist could make a peace pact.

The Bible indicates this Antichrist's powerful takeover transpires after the Rapture.ᵐ The world acceptance of his control comes because of his promises of universal peace.ⁿ According to prophecy he actually draws up a treaty guaranteeing peace to Israel. Unfortunately, this long-awaited hope of peace is soon shattered as this evil,

---

ʲ Jeremiah 16:14, 15

ᵏ As per telephone conversation, June 1991, with Rabbi Wexler, Dean of University of Judaism Los Angeles, CA.

ˡ *See* Isaiah 18:3, 27:13, 58:1-14, and the book of Joel.

ᵐ II Thessalonians 2:3-9

ⁿ Revelation 6:1, 2 and all of chapter 13

satanically-led dictator breaks the treaty after three and one-half years and attempts to annihilate the unsuspecting Jews.[o]

Preparation for Treaty

One needs only to read any issue of the *Jerusalem Post* to recognize the growing fear among European Jews as to their safety. The warnings of seasoned sufferers of prejudice caution that the growing undercurrent of Anti-Semitism both in Europe and elsewhere is leading to another "holocaust."

As Israeli leaders struggle with the problems of housing shortages, inflation, and jobless citizens, "Aliya"[p] continues. The frantic immigration in 1990 alone moved 200,000 Jews to this tiny country. The Israeli government projects the return of 400,000 to 600,000 in 1991 which is based in part on Jewry's recognition and fear of the smoldering Anti-Semitic danger worldwide.

It's noteworthy to recognize that most Gentiles are not supportive of Israel nor (historically) have Jews been very welcome in Gentile nations. How interesting to note that the people who are the exceptions to the ongoing criticism and abuse of Jews are mostly pre-millennial, evangelical Christians.[q67]

Most likely, when authentic Christians leave in the Rapture, **there will be no safe country, no safe place left for the Jews of the world, except Israel!** This heavenly withdrawal of a host of Jewish supporters only compounds the dangers of both worldwide Anti-Semitism and the

---

[o] Daniel 9:27; Revelation 12:13-17

[p] Term for Jewish immigration to Israel.

[q] This point is mentioned even by the Jews themselves in comments in the *Jerusalem Post*. They comment that those who take a literal interpretation of the Bible as opposed to an allegorical approach comprise the bulk of the Christian support for Jews.

historic Arab-Israeli conflict. This unstable condition arising from multiple problems will pave the way for Jewish acceptance of a world peace treaty.

Interesting Jewish Insights Concerning Rosh HaShanah

Rabbis emphasize the joyous character of Rosh HaShanah as well as its solemnity.[68] Three stages of judgment are seen by Jewish scholars: "Three books are opened on Rosh HaShanah, one for the wicked, one for the righteous, and one for the in-between. The righteous are immediately inscribed in the book of life, the wicked in the book of death, and the verdict of the in-between is suspended until Yom Kippur."[69] The scriptural origin of this belief comes from God's statement, *"And I will cause you to pass under the rod, and I will bring you into the land of the covenant."*[r]

Could the righteous people they see be the believers, both Jewish and Gentile, who are taken up in the Rapture? Since Rosh HaShanah is a harvest festival, this day may well represent the harvest of souls taken up to heaven. Remember at Firstfruits four months earlier, one sheaf was waved but it is referred to both in Leviticus and I Corinthians in the **plural**. *"Christ the firstfruits; afterward they that are Christ's at His coming."*[s] Using the plural makes the picture complete. Firstfruits represented Jesus first, then it represents all believers for whom He provides His righteousness and salvation.

---

[r] Ezekiel 20:37. The reference to "passing under the rod" comes from the shepherd's practice of sorting the sheep that come into the fold at night as the sheep pass under the shepherd's rod.

[s] I Corinthians 15:23

Perhaps the wicked who are inscribed in the book of the dead, are those referred to in the book of Revelation as having taken the mark of the beast during Tribulation. *"And all that dwell upon the earth shall worship him, whose names are not written in the book of life of the Lamb slain from the foundation of the world." "And the smoke of their torment ascendeth up for ever and ever: and they have no rest day nor night, who worship the beast and his image, and whosoever receiveth the mark of his name." "And they that dwell on the earth shall wonder, whose names were not written in the book of life from the foundation of the world."*[t]

Maybe the last group referred to as the "in-betweens" are those who do not take the mark of the beast, and will (during or at the end of the seven years of Tribulation) at last believe in Jesus Christ as Messiah![u]

REVIEW OF FEAST OF TRUMPETS
(ROSH HASHANAH)

The all-day blowing of trumpets ushered in this Jewish feast day. This first day of the Jewish year is celebrated as a solemn day of gathering, examination by God, and confounding of Satan. The last trumpet blast of this Rosh HaShanah gathering beautifully describes the focal point of Christian hope, the Rapture!

---

[t] Revelation 13:8, 14:11, 17:8

[u] Zechariah 12:8:10; Revelation 7:3-8, 14:1-5

CHAPTER 8
DAY OF ATONEMENT (Feast #6)

SPRING				FALL	
NISAN 14	NISAN 15	SUN. AFTER SABBATH	50 DAYS LATER	TISHRI 1	TISHRI 10
Preparation for Passover	Unleavened Dinner	Firstfruits, Resurrection	Weeks, Pentecost	Trumpets, Rapture	Atonement, 2nd coming

The most solemn holy day of the Jews today is known as Yom Kippur. On this day, the ordinary transactions of life in Israel stop completely. The deserted streets and closed switchboards demonstrate that all the people have only one thought in mind, the celebration of Yom Kippur.

As originally given by God, the ritual could begin only after the high priest offered a bullock as a sin offering for himself and his family. God then instructed him to select two goats. By a drawing of lots, one was selected as a sacrifice offering for the sins of the nation of Israel. The high priest carried the blood of this goat into the Holy of Holies and sprinkled it on and in front of the Mercy Seat.

The nation waited in hushed anticipation as their high priest came out of the holy place and sprinkled the blood of the bullock and the goat upon the horns of the altar seven times. If the priest lived through the whole ritual, the nation knew God had forgiven them for one more year!

Next, the high priest called for the second goat, placed his hands on its head, and confessed over it the sins of the nation. A priest then led it out to the wilderness and let it go.[a] This scapegoat, called "Azazel" in Hebrew, figuratively bore the sins of the people.

The Jews traditionally ended this solemn celebration by a blowing of the shofar horn called "Shofar haGadol" or "The Great Trumpet." This blowing symbolized not only the end of the ceremony, but gaiety, since the national, yearly sacrifice had been accepted.[70]

Victor Buksbazen writes in *The Gospel in the Feasts of Israel*, that the Jews believe, "On Yom Kippur God seals the books of accounting which have been opened on New Year's Day. Whereas before on New Year's Day, (Rosh HaShanah) Jews wish one another that their name be "inscribed" into the book of life, in the days leading up to the Day of Atonement, when greeting one another or sending greetings in writing, the word is 'may you be sealed in the book of life.'"[71] Although the Day of Atonement is the tenth day of the seventh month, the preceding seven days have become connected to this feast. These seven days are called by the Jews, "The Days of Affliction" or "The Days of Awe."

On the first day of these seven (the third of Tishri), the Fast of Gedaliah is observed. The next observance during these seven days is called "Shabbat Shuvah," which is held on the Sabbath (Saturday) of this week. The last special day of these seven Days of Awe, is called "Erev Yom Kippur" or Yom Kippur Eve. Instructions for Yom Kippur command the Jews to *"afflict your souls by a statute forever."*[b]

The Jews today still afflict themselves on Erev Yom Kippur. They confess their sins and recite, "For He is merciful and forgives iniquity." Only after this total week of soul-searching does the all-important Day of Atonement begin.

---

[a] Leviticus 16:1-34

[b] Leviticus 16:29-31 Jews believe this is God's appointed time to become introspective and search for any sins yet unconfessed. Some Jews even have interpreted this instruction to mean physical flagellation.

Handling the Loss of the Temple

The biblical guidelines for Yom Kippur were observed by the Jews as long as they had the tabernacle or the temple in which to properly offer the sacrifices. After the destruction of Herod's Temple in A.D. 70, the Jews faced the question of how to celebrate this religious service.

The rabbinic leadership experienced tremendous shock as a result of losing their temple. The depth of their loss is reflected in their dismal words. "Now that we have no prophet or Kohen or sacrifice, who shall atone for us? The only thing left to us is prayer."[72]

They also say, "Prayer was a natural substitute for the sacrificial offerings...Subsequently, the rabbis added two more keys to salvation, **essential to winning God's mercies on Yom Kippur.**"[c]

"Said Rabbi Eliezer[d]: 'Three elements avert a harsh decree, they are—prayer, charity, and penitence.'"[73]

They base these three replacement choices on Hosea 12:2,3 and Nehemiah 8:9.

It's amazing to see the direction this theology has taken the Jewish beliefs which, as you will see, is far afield from the original design of Yom Kippur. **Confession of sin to God, and a God-ordained substitutionary blood sacrifice has been replaced by a man-centered, good works system of appeasement toward God.**

This drastic shift is substantiated by a contemporary Jewish theologian who writes, "The rabbinic three keys to salvation emphasized the social aspects of Yom Kippur. Whereas the previous sacrificial motif of the fast was mainly God-directed, the rabbinic orientation gave concrete emphasis to the prophetic admonitions that man's

---

[c] Emphasis mine.

[d] Respected second century Rabbi.

protestations of piety are not acceptable to God if his sense of social justice is faulty. To obtain divine forgiveness, one must not only make peace with God, but also man. The attainment of peace, individual and communal, thus became a prime objective of Yom Kippur. It is in this spirit that Rabbi Eleazar[e] declared: 'Great peace, for **even if Israel is worshiping idols,**[f]'if they keep the peace and are united, they will be spared the judgment of the Almighty'(Pesikta Rabbati)."[74]

This works-centered justification system is certainly in contradiction to the Jews' own commentary on the Bible, the Talmud. It states, *"There is no atonement except with blood."*[75]

A detailed reading of the sacrificial rites was incorporated as part of the Yom Kippur liturgy. Still today, these three elements of prayer, charity, and penitence are the replacements for the once-a-year national blood sacrifice. Only the ritual of Kapparot retains any semblance to the original Yom Kippur sacrifices. Some Orthodox Jews select a chicken, preferably white, and recite, "A life for a life." After prayers and a laying of their right hand upon the head of the "kapparah," they swing this live chicken over their head and say, "This is my substitute, this is my exchange, this is my atonement. This fowl will go to death, and I shall enter upon a good and long life and peace." After three repetitions of this ceremony the chicken is slaughtered.[76]

The loss of the temple and the opportunity to offer sacrifice to God brought the Jews to a fork in the road. They could take the path of redesigning their approach to God, or follow the other road by asking themselves the question, "If God has allowed the destruction of our only place of sacrifice, has He perhaps already provided the promised sacrifice of Isaiah 53?"

---

[e] A contemporary of Rabbi Eliezer.

[f] Emphasis mine.

The Ultimate Prophecy

Hundreds of prophecies in the Tanakh[g] pointed to Jesus as the ultimate messianic sacrifice. Isaiah chapter 53 typifies this information. But even beyond the Old Testament prophecies and the flawless life of Jesus, God gave another messianic indicator. This phenomenon was directly related to the temple worship and particularly to Yom Kippur.

Between the Holy Place and the Holy of Holies hung an elaborate curtain called "the veil." Its name in Hebrew means "to hide or cover." This blue, purple, and scarlet veil of fine-twined, byssus linen, glittered with the woven-gold figures of cherubim. The purpose of the veil was two-fold. Besides shielding the Holy of Holies from all but the high priest, this veil covered the Ark whenever the Jews relocated[h] their portable temple[i].

J. Vernon McGee comments on the veil in *The Tabernacle: God's Portrait of Christ* "It protected the holiness of God, whether on the wilderness march or when it was in its place in the tabernacle. It protected the holiness of God from the profanity of man. It protected both God and man.

"When the temple of Solomon was erected, the veil was perpetuated in the temple, only it was larger and more elaborate. It was a beautiful work of art, gorgeous in design, artistic in color, superb in the minutest detail, and rich in adornment... Josephus tells us that it was **four inches thick** in his day and renewed each year. **Wild horses tied to each**

---

[g] All of the Old Testament.

[h] Numbers 4:5

[i] Known as The Tabernacle and used from Moses until Solomon.

end of the veil, after it had been taken down, were not able to rend it asunder."[j] [77]

A cascade of astonishing phenomena struck Jerusalem at the exact moment of Jesus' death. An earthquake shook the city. Rocks split apart. Inside the temple, though, an even more awesome event, heavy with significance, touched the veil. This curtain, four inches thick, was **ripped from top to bottom** by an unseen hand.

Matthew solemnly describes this awesome event. *"Jesus, when he had cried again with a loud voice, yielded up the ghost. And, behold the veil of the temple was rent in twain from the top to the bottom; and the earth did quake, and the rocks rent."[k]*

The veil no longer separated the people from the Holy of Holies. What did this mean? What about Yom Kippur? God answers these questions by explaining that Jesus became the *"once for all"* Yom Kippur sacrifice. God promises, *"By one offering he hath perfected for ever them that are sanctified...And their sins and iniquities will I remember no more...Now where remission of these is, there is no more offering for sin...Having therefore, brethren, boldness to enter into the holiest by the blood of Jesus,...By a new and living way, which he hath consecrated for us, through the veil, that is to say, his flesh."[l]*

This veil had been a forerunner, an Old Testament picture of Jesus Christ. For fifteen hundred years, access to the glory and forgiveness of God had been provided only one way, via a priest, through the veil. God ripped the veil in half at the moment of Jesus' death. As on previous Yom Kippurs, God accepted the sacrifice, but this time it was forever. It never needed to be repeated again. Jesus became

---

[j] This actually took place in A.D. 70. The Roman army destroyed everything in the temple and leveled the building leaving not even a brick standing.

[k] Matthew 27:50, 51

[l] Hebrews 10:10, 14, 17-22

the access to God, so the separating curtain was replaced by the Holy Person of the Godhead whom it represented.

Some Jews and some Gentiles recognized the fulfillment of Old Testament prophecy in the person of Jesus Christ. Most did not. History and the rabbinical teachings demonstrate a choice to refuse God's plan which offered Jesus as fulfilling the need for the shedding of innocent blood. Instead they invented a works system of approach to God.

Certainly the Jews are not alone in the attempt to approach God on the basis of their deeds instead of on the basis of the substitutionary sacrifice of Jesus. Mankind at large makes the same exchange by the religions which they design. Sadly a works system is even taught by many who claim the name of "Christian."

God reaffirmed the Old Testament teaching concerning the absolute necessity of a blood sacrifice. He stated in the New Testament, "*Without the shedding of blood there is no remission of sins.*" How sad that today numbers of so-called Christians as well as many Jews find the references to blood sacrifice "barbaric."

Solemn words from God warn us about this independent attitude. "*There is a way that seemeth right unto man, but the end thereof are the ways of death.*"[m] Oh how much need there is for each one of us to say the words of Acts 5:29, "*We ought to obey God rather than man.*"

Yom Kippur's Picture

God commanded concerning Yom Kippur, "*And this shall be an everlasting statute unto you, to make an atonement for the children of Israel for all their sin once a year.*"[n]

---

[m] Proverbs 16:25

[n] Leviticus 7:25

Just before the prophetic picture (Isaiah 53) of the Messiah who would die for the sins of the nation, another picture of Yom Kippur occurs. Isaiah prophesies, "*As many were astonished at thee; his visage was so marred more than any man, and his form more than the sons of men; so shall he sprinkle many nations.*"[o] This mention of "sprinkling" is a direct reference to the sprinkling on the altar done by the high priest on Yom Kippur.

Believers in Jesus Christ, who have studied the New Testament, understand that the high priest's job of representing the nation was an early picture of the Great High Priest, Jesus Christ. The book of Hebrews in a reference to Jesus, promises, "*Wherefore he is able to save them to the uttermost that come unto God by him, seeing he ever liveth to make intercession for them.*

For such an high priest became us, who is holy, harmless, undefiled, separate from sinners, and made higher than the heavens;

Who needeth not daily, as those high priests, to offer up sacrifices, first for his own sins, and then for the people's: for this he did once, when he offered up himself."[p]

The typology or picture concerning the Day of Atonement is further explained in Hebrews chapter 9.

The two goats used on Yom Kippur present a beautiful picture of Jesus. One goat had to die (as Jesus had to die) while the other goat lived and carried the sins of the people into the wilderness and disappeared. Jesus, as our living Savior, carries our sins, and God removes them from us, "*As far as the east is from the west.*"[q]

It grieves us to discover that the observance of this feast was changed by the Jews sometime after the specifics

---

o   Isaiah 52:14, 15

p   Hebrews 7:25-27

q   Psalm 103:12

had been given to them by God. By the second temple period,[r] they were pulling hair out of the scapegoat and shouting angrily as it was led past them on the way to the desert. How amazing that this anger toward the goat, that was bearing their sins, so reflects the behavior of many Jews as Jesus was arrested, tried, and crucified for the sins of the world.

Strangely, someone designed a new ending to the ceremony of Yom Kippur. Jewish historian Theodor Gaster tells us the scapegoat, marked by a crimson thread, walked alongside a chosen priest to a ravine located twelve miles outside Jerusalem. Standing at the edge of the precipice, the priest divided the red thread, tying one part to a rock and the other between the horns of the goat. "Then he pushed the animal from behind till it went rolling down, 'and' says the Mishna, 'ere it reached half-way, it was broken to pieces.'"[78]

As we know, today the Jews do not have a living Savior. The prophetic importance in Yom Kippur is seen in both the original guidelines as given by God and in the changes the Jews instituted.

Another Tragic Change

God gave exact guidelines to Moses describing the dimensions for the tabernacle as well as the objects to place inside. According to God's guidelines, the inner court, as well as the Holy of Holies, had no windows.[s] Priests could see to officiate within the inner court from the light provided by a golden lampstand. This light was to be kept burning continually.

---

[r] 515 B.C.

[s] J. Vernon McGee p. 75 The Tabernacle God's Portrait of Christ.

The Holy of Holies, however not only had no source of outside light, it also had no physical provision of light inside. The only object of furniture it contained was the Ark of the Covenant. This wooden box, covered inside and out with gold, contained a pot of manna,[t] Aaron's rod that budded, and the stone tablets of law.[u] The Mercy Seat of pure gold rested on the top, over which two golden cherubims hovered, with wings outstretched.

(The significance of these objects as prepictures of Jesus Christ being the access to God is beautifully portrayed in J. Vernon McGee's book, *The Tabernacle: God's Portrait of Christ*.)

The Bible explains that after the craftsmen under Moses finished the tabernacle, *"The glory of the Lord filled the tabernacle."*[v] Because of God's light, the high priest could see to carry out the yearly ritual of Yom Kippur.

This light of God is intricately involved with the Ark itself as demonstrated when the Ark was stolen by the Philistines. *"The glory is departed from Israel: because the ark of God was taken."*[w] Not too surprisingly, after the Philistines were devastated by disease because they possessed the ark, and the Bethshemites lost 50,070 men for looking inside, the Ark was gladly returned. The Ark eventually rested in the permanent version of the tabernacle, known as Solomon's Temple. Once again, God provided His light in The Holy of Holies.[x]

---

[t] Food that God provided the Jews during the forty year wandering in the desert.

[u] Hebrews 9:4, 5

[v] Exodus 40:34, 35

[w] I Samuel 4:21

[x] I Kings 8:11

Unfortunately, the Jews slowly ceased to worship and obey God which brought about the withdrawal of God's glory from the temple and their eventual expulsion from the Promised Land.[y]

Babylonians destroyed Solomon's Temple in 587 B.C.[z] A second temple built by Jews in 515 B.C., was refurbished and greatly enlarged, by Herod the Great in 19 B.C. This elaborate and enormous structure covered forty acres and took decades to complete. Jewish sources say the Holy of Holies in this temple remained empty, apparently never possessing the ark.[79] Consequently, the glory of God never resided in this temple!

The Tragic Change Occurs

Now let's look at the aforementioned, tragic change in Yom Kippur. The *Encyclopedia Judaica* records a short statement containing profound implications. It states that on the three pilgrim festivals (which would include Yom Kippur) "the curtain which normally hung at the entrance to the sanctuary, was rolled up to enable the people to view the Holy of Holies."[80]

The tragedy of this revelation is that not only did the Jews commit a sacrilege by looking inside the sanctuary, they state the reason they lifted the curtain was so the people outside could see in. Could it be that the lone candelabra no longer gave sufficient light for the priests to officiate? What a tragedy! Even though the glory of God

---

[y] Ezekiel 10:18-19

[z] J. Vernon McGee mentions the "ensign" that will come from Ethiopia (referred to in Isaiah 18:3) is a possible reference to the Ark of the Covenant *Isaiah vol. I* p.141.

Grant Jeffrey discusses in chapter VIII of his book, *Heaven The Last Frontier*, the possibility that the Ark in Solomom's Temple was only a replica. He suggests that a secret exchange took place and that the original Ark was known to be absent from the second temple. He also presents a fascinating scenario describing Ethiopia as the present location of the authentic Ark.

had long since departed, neither the people nor the priests noticed that God was no longer a part of this ceremony. On Yom Kippur, what mercy could the high priest hope to find for his nation in the dark and empty Holy of Holies?

This picture of turning from God, and not recognizing that His power had departed is reminiscent of Samson's experience. After Samson turned his back on God and gave in to Delilah's pleadings to tell her the secret of his strength, the Bible says, "*He wist not that the Lord was departed from him.*"[aa]

It's no wonder that the Pharisees who possessed this same spiritual blindness were referred to by Jesus as "*blind guides*" and "*whited sepulchres...full of dead men's bones.*"[bb]

More Meaning

The Jewish custom of ten days of "Teshuvah"[cc] begins on Rosh HaShanah and ends on Yom Kippur. Within this time their seven Days of Affliction present us with even more prophetic significance. Remember, beginning on the third of Tishri, the Fast of Gedaliah transpires. Nobel Prize-winner S.Y. Agnon tells us in *Days of Awe*,"Conscientious readers go into seclusion for seven days beginning with the Fast of Gedaliah until Yom Kippur, and study the order of service and mend their deeds and seclude themselves to be alone with their Maker night and day in solitude and piety, as the high priest used to do."[81]

Note another aspect of Jewish teaching concerning the Days of Awe. "The Sabbath between Rosh HaShanah

---

[aa] Judges 16:20

[bb] Matthew 23:24, 27

[cc] This Jewish belief defines a time of intense introspection when the sinner tries to recall all his sin, forsake it, and remove it from his thoughts concluding never to do it again. If he is faithful in his repentance, he will be forgiven on Yom Kippur.

and Yom Kippur is called the 'Sabbath of Return,' because then the portion from the Prophets beginning 'Return O Israel, unto the Lord thy God' (Hosea 14:2) is read."[82]

It is very possible that the seven days during which the Jews prepare themselves spiritually for the Great Day of Atonement is God's picture of the seven-year great Tribulation.

Another correlation of Yom Kippur and the day of recognition of Jesus as Messiah is seen in the writing of a Jewish rabbi. Philip Goodman records an amazing act which ends this seven-day observance. On this last day (which is the Day of Atonement) the participants pronounce the "ineffable[dd] name of God" and bow the knee at the feeling of God's nearness. **"Here and only here does the Jew kneel...The congregation prostrates itself before the King Of Kings."**[ee][83]

We know God promises in the Old and New Testaments that on some future day every knee will bow before Him,[ff] but how meaningful this observance becomes when the light of Philippians 2:10 shines upon it: *"That at the name of Jesus every knee shall bow."* Yes, even the current observances of Jews reveal that much is already in place for national recognition of their Messiah, Jesus, on **some** Yom Kippur.

It is actually taught by the Jews that because of this face-to-face confrontation with God, the Jewish idiom for Yom Kippur became **"face to face"**![84] Do not those words simply leap out at us? In the light of a Jewish perspective of

---

[dd] Unutterable, never to be spoken except at this time.

[ee] Emphasis mine.

[ff] Isaiah 45:22-25; Romans 14:11

Yom Kippur we can savor the words, "*For now we see through a glass darkly; but then <u>face to face</u>.*"[88]

The Great Trumpet Blast

The ceremonies of Yom Kippur close with the trumpet blast called Shofar haGadol. This great blast sounds upon the "closing of the gate" ceremony which formally ends Yom Kippur. How like God's words, "*And it shall come to pass in that day, that <u>the great trumpet</u> shall be blown, and they shall come which were ready to perish in the land of Assyria, and the outcasts which were ready to perish in the land of Assyria, and the outcasts in the land of Egypt, and shall worship the Lord in the holy mount at Jerusalem.*"[hh] God's word reveals information that ties in a great trumpet blast with the total regathering of the Jews to Israel and the Second Coming of Jesus.[ii]

During this present church age, the Lord has been dealing directly with mankind as a whole, rather than through the Jewish nation. After the Rapture of the church (comprised of believing Gentiles and Jews), God will once again turn His spotlight on the nation of the Jews. God plans, through these seven years, to bring the Jews to a spiritual condition in which they at last recognize Jesus as their Messiah. I believe Yom Kippur will be the exact time that the Jews as a nation, finally believe in the saving power of Jesus. This future turning to God is described in chapters 12 and 14 of Zechariah. "*And I will pour out upon the house of David, and upon the inhabitants of Jerusalem, the spirit of grace and of supplication: and they shall look upon me whom they have*

---

[88] I Corinthians 13:12

[hh] Isaiah 27:13. Although Jewish writers connect this verse to Rosh HaShanah, the correct application of this Scripture can only be made when Jesus is recognized as Messiah.

[ii] See Isaiah 18:3, 58:1; Joel 2:1, 15; Matthew 24:31

pierced, and they shall mourn for him, as one mourneth for his only son, and shall be in bitterness for him as one that is in bitterness for his firstborn."[ij]

How fitting that Jewish custom teaches that this holy day is the time a person's name can be sealed in the Book of Life!

REVIEW OF THE DAY OF ATONEMENT (YOM KIPPUR)

The most solemn feast of the seven listed in Leviticus, is the Day of Atonement. On this day, known as Yom Kippur, hangs the fate of the whole nation of Israel. The high priest enters the Holy of Holies to offer a sacrifice for the sins of the nation. If the sacrifice is accepted by God, then the nation of Jews rejoices because they have been given another year to live.

Since the loss of the temple in A.D. 70, it has been impossible to celebrate this feast according to God's original design.

One gazes in amazement at the awesome picture of redemption contained in Yom Kippur. Jesus Christ, as mankind's great High Priest, entered the Holy of Holies in heaven to present His sacrificial blood to God the Father. God's acceptance of this offering provided eternal salvation for all who trust in Christ's sacrifice.

[ij] Zechariah 12:10

CHAPTER 9
FEAST OF TABERNACLES (Feast #7)

SPRING				FALL		
NISAN 14	NISAN 15	SUN. AFTER SABBATH	50 DAYS LATER	TISHRI 1	TISHRI 10	TISHRI 15
Preparation for Passover	Unleavened Dinner	Firstfruits, Resurrection	Weeks, Pentecost	Trumpets, Rapture	Atonement, 2nd coming	Tabernacles, Millennium

Succoth, or Festival of Tabernacles (Booths), is an eight day time of joyous commemoration. At this time the Jews remember and thank the Lord for the provisions He gave them after they were rescued from bondage in Egypt.

According to the instructions in Leviticus chapter 23, the Jews celebrated this feast by building booths of palm, willow, and other thick branches. They still do this today. On each of first seven days, special offerings are burned on the altar.[85] Later, they added the ceremonies of the pouring of water and the lighting of four huge elevated lamps in the temple courtyard. These symbols reminded the Jews of God's provision of water in the wilderness and of His pillar of fire that guided them by night. Four huge oil-burning vats actually beamed shafts of light across the whole city of Jerusalem.

The water-pouring ceremony, repeated on each of the seven days, brought such great joy to the people that Succoth became known as "the season of our joy." The celebrants each brought an "etrog" or citron—the yellow citrus fruit that is about the same size as a lemon, but sweeter and spicier. Besides bringing this fruit as suggested in Leviticus, the jubilant participants wove branches of palm, myrtle, and willow into a large fan called a "lulav."

Meanwhile the priests divided themselves into three large groups, each group heading in a different direction. One group set off to Bethlehem to purchase animals for the day's sacrifice. Another group traveled in procession from the temple to a place below Jerusalem called Motza where they cut off willow branches. These priests returned in a long line, all waving these tall limbs back and forth. The third contingent of priests exited through the water gate taking with them a golden flagon. The high priest dipped out three measures of water from the pool of Siloam then returned leading his group of priests.

Back in Time

Calling this festival "season of our joy" can readily be understood when we take ourselves back in time for a moment to listen and observe this awesome spectacle...

Look at the long line of priests,
hundreds of them, threading through the
water gate and winding down to the pool of
Siloam. More priests curl through the narrow
streets on the way to Bethlehem to secure the
special sacrifices. Gaze across the holy city and
see hundreds of thousands of Jewish pilgrims
lining the streets waving their lulavs. Not to
be overlooked, watch the column of priests
waving their huge willow branches as they
return through the eastern gate to the temple.

The sound, oh the glorious sound. Hear
the heavenly sound of the flute. Listen to the
Levites on the temple steps. How many are
there? They're playing flutes and lyres,
cymbals and trumpets. Oh the joy! Listen to

the people! Hear them singing the words of
the psalms. *"Praise ye the Lord. Blessed is the
man that feareth the Lord...This is the Lord's doing;
it is marvelous in our eyes. This is the day which
the Lord hath made; we will rejoice and be glad in
it."*ᵃ

The climactic ending came each day when the three
lines of priests converged at the altar. First they placed the
sacrifices upon the altar. Next the willow-bearing priests
placed their cut branches around the altar forming a circle
that canopied the animals. Last the high priest, carrying the
golden flagon of water, ascended the steps leading to the
altar. Connected to the altar, were two plaster, funnel-
shaped bowls with tubes below that ran back into the altar.
Each day's ceremony ended with the high priest pouring his
measures of water into the bowl while his assistant poured
measures of wine into the other bowl.[86]

Beginning one month before Rosh HaShanah (forty
days before Yom Kippur), the worship and study of the
Scriptures led up to these ceremonies. Every Scripture in
these studies related to water and light, keeping the
symbolism fresh in everyone's mind. They heard words
such as, *"Behold God is my salvation; I will trust and not be
afraid; for the Lord JEHOVAH is my strength and my song; he
also is become my salvation. Therefore with joy shall ye draw
water out of the wells of salvation."*ᵇ

Can't you feel the electricity and utter amazement of
the thousands gathered in the temple courtyard on the day
that Jesus attended the Feast of Tabernacles? Imagine, He
called out to the crowd, "*If any man thirst, let him come to Me,
and drink. He that believeth on Me, as the scripture hath said, out*

ᵃ Psalms 112-118 were sung at Passover, Firstfruits and Tabernacles.

ᵇ Isaiah 12:2, 3

of his belly shall flow rivers of living water."[c]   He used this
ceremony of the pouring of the water, to offer His beloved
people the salvation He had come to provide.

Doesn't the pouring out of the water and the wine
remind us of the ultimate price of love Jesus paid for us on
the cross? Remember one of the soldiers *"pierced his side, and
forthwith came out blood and water."*[d] He used this celebration
which pictured Him so beautifully, not just in the water
pouring but also in the branches,[e] then in the lambs, the
rams, the bulls, and the goat, to reach out in love to His
people.

At the end of this feast on its eighth day, Jesus again
stunned the Pharisees when He used their ritual celebration
of lights to teach that He was the Messiah. Standing in the
very same courtyard that held the four great lights, he
proclaimed, *"I am the light of the world: he that followeth me shall
not walk in darkness, but shall have the light of life."*[f]

From the Past to the Future

In the Bible we discover that Solomon chose the Feast
of Tabernacles to dedicate the first temple.[g] This day of the
year seems to be selected by God as his special time of
consecration. The representation of Jesus in Feast of
Tabernacles comes alive to us in a Jewish prayer repeated
during the celebration. This petition added to the grace said
after meals, asks, "May the All-merciful raise up for us the

---

[c] John 7:2, 10, 37-39

[d] John 19:34

[e] Isaiah 4:2; 11:1

[f] John 8:12

[g] I Kings 8:1-5; II Chronicles 7:8-10

fallen tabernacle (*succah*) of David."[87] A contemporary Jewish
Rabbi comments on this ancient prayer, "We ask for the
restoration of the Davidic Kingdom, the Messianic Age."[88]

We see pictures of Jesus in this beautiful Jewish
Succoth poem. It describes the remembrance of past
provision in the wilderness as well as future hope of a
Messianic Kingdom age.

Thy cloud enfolded them, as if that they
Were shelter'd in a booth; redeem'd and free,
They saw Thy glory as a canopy
Spread o'er them as they marched upon their way

And when dryshod they through the sea had gone,
They praised Thee and proclaimed Thy unity;
And all the angels sang the antiphon,
And lifted up their voices unto Thee.
"Our Rock, our Savior He"—thus did they sing—
"World without end, the Lord shall reign as King!"[89]

Fulfillment of Tabernacles

Most Bible scholars are agreed on the future
fulfillment of the Feast of Tabernacles. This is the
Millennium![h] Jesus Christ will reign from Jerusalem. The
whole world will look to the Jews for knowledge of the
Lord.[i] Zechariah describes this exciting time for us. "*And it
shall come to pass, that every one that is left of all the nations
which came against Jerusalem shall even go up from year to year to
worship the King, the Lord of hosts, and to keep the feast of
tabernacles.*"[j]

---

[h] Revelation 20:4-6

[i] Zechariah 8:23

[j] Zechariah 14:16, see also verses 4, 9

From the sacred writings of the Jews we read these amazing words that describe the rehearsal for this coming era. "The people said to the nations of the earth: Because of us, the Holy One blessed be He, does all these [good] things for you, and yet you hate us...At the Festival of Tabernacles we offer up seventy bullocks [as an atonement] for the seventy nations, and we pray that rain will come down for them."[90]

How fascinating to note in a previously quoted passage of Hosea[k], that not only is a time of two thousand years of judgment indicated for the Jewish nation, but this passage also infers that afterwards, a one-thousand-year peaceful reign of Messiah will transpire for the Jews. The passage states, *"After two days will he revive us: in the third day he will raise us up, and we shall live in his sight."*

REVIEW OF FEAST OF TABERNACLES (SUCCOTH)

Celebrating Tabernacles in Israel produces jubilation throughout their land. Festivities surround this remembrance of God's provision during the wandering in the wilderness and the future hope of a messianic kingdom of peace. Each family enjoys the relaxation in the booths of branches built on their rooftops[l] and balconies or in their yards.

The prophetic masterpiece, painted by God in the Feast of Tabernacles is none other than the peaceful, future one thousand year reign of Jesus Christ.

---

[k] Hosea 5:12-6:3

[l] Rooftops in this region are traditionally flat which enables the home owners to utilize their roofs for various purposes.

SUMMARY OF FEASTS

Pesach (Nisan 14)	Passover CRUCIFIXION	Each family sacrifices one lamb in remembrance of their rescue from bondage in Egypt. This feast was fulfilled by the sacrifice of JESUS CHRIST.
Hag-Ha-Matzot (Nisan 15)	Unleavened Bread PURGING SIN	All leaven is taken from the home during this week-long feast. The penalty of sin (represented by leaven) was taken from mankind and placed on JESUS CHRIST.
Bikkurim (Sun. after Sat. after Passover)	Firstfruits RESURRECTION	A sheaf of grain from the first yearly harvest is offered to the Lord. On Easter morning came the discovery of the first one ever to be resurrected from the dead, JESUS CHRIST.
Shavout (50 days after Firstfruits)	Feast of Weeks PENTECOST	Another harvest sacrifice offered to the Lord was two loaves baked with leaven. The promised Holy Spirit came and indwelt believers (both Jewish and Gentile). This combined group is called the Church or body of JESUS CHRIST.
— (Four month gap) — Rosh HaShanah (Tishri 1)	Trumpets RAPTURE	A day of judgment and gathering which was announced by an all-day blowing of trumpets. The hope of all believers is the Rapture when they will be taken up into heaven by none other than JESUS CHRIST.
Yom Kippur (Tishri 15)	Atonement Day SECOND COMING	On this solemn day the high priest offered a sacrifice for the sins of the nation. A one-time sacrifice for all mankind was made by the High Priest, JESUS CHRIST.
Succoth (Tishri 15)	Tabernacles MILLENNIUM	This festive celebration commemorated God's provision in the past and His promised Messianic Kingdom of the future. The coming Millennium of peace will be ruled over by the coming King, JESUS CHRIST.

After observing the prophetic meaning of all seven Jewish feasts, the Hebrew definition of "feasts" becomes quite real to us. These feasts really are "appointments." Appointments not just with God, but appointments with Jesus. **The Jewish Feasts are Jesus Feasts!**

✡ ✡ ✡ ✡ ✡ ✡

SECTION IV
PROHIBITIONS TO SPECIFIC DATING

The first four feasts of Israel describe in detail (including the timing) events connected with Christ's first coming. The remaining three feasts appear also to give details concerning His future Second Coming **even to exact days!** Information this specific stands in direct contradiction to our traditional understanding of "date-setting."

Most Christians concur that it is useless to search for **exact dates** of end time occurrences. Reason dictates that it's foolish to try to determine the exact date of a biblical future event such as the Rapture, when the Bible itself states one cannot know the exact date.

A representative statement of the orthodox approach to "date setting" is found in *Bible Prophecy*, by Charles J. Woodbridge.

"THE TIME OF CHRIST'S COMING
1. Due Caution
No man knows the exact hour of Jesus' return (Matthew 24:36,42). History tells us that occasionally people have forgotten or ignored our Savior's warning words. They have set dates for His return, put their affairs in order for an early departure from earth, and gathered at appointed centers to meet the Lord. Informed Christians however, know better than this. They always keep their affairs in order. They delight in anticipating Christ's return. But they are extremely careful not to set dates.

2. The Swift Immediacy of His Coming

Jesus will come *suddenly,* 'in a moment, in the twinkling of an eye' (I Corinthians 15:52). As the lightning flash (Matthew 24:27), or an unexpected thief (Matthew 24:43), or a snare (Luke 21:35), so will Christ's coming be. Think through each one of these comparisons. How rapid is the twinkling of an eye or a flash of lightning? How suddenly does a thief steal and then escape? How unexpectedly and quickly does a snare seize it's prey?"[91]

As you see, these words from Woodbridge reflect the position of most theologians. This viewpoint is pervasive and has had longevity. However, in light of the **specific prophetic fulfillments of numerous Jewish celebrations,** a review of the dating prohibition is in order.

CHAPTER 10
THIEF IN THE NIGHT

One of the Bible verses used to explain this uselessness of specific dating is I Thessalonians 5:2, *"The day of the Lord so cometh as a thief in the night."* The interpretation of this Scripture has always been, "Since one does not know when a thief is coming, one also cannot know when the Rapture will occur."

The first time I remotely considered reviewing any of these Scriptures was in 1974. My spouse asked me the intriguing question, "Why do we Christians use I Thessalonians 5:2 to prove we can't date the Rapture, when verse four, only two verses later says, *'But ye brethren, are not in darkness, that that day should overtake you as a thief'?"* I couldn't answer.

Another "thief" passage from Revelation 3:3, with a similar ending is, *"Remember therefore how thou hast received and heard, and hold fast, and repent. If therefore thou shalt not watch, I will come on thee as a thief, and thou shalt not know what hour I will come upon thee."* Again, it appeared that both of these "thief" Scriptures taught that Christians should not be surprised to see Jesus.

In 1975 we asked a noted prophetic author about the Thessalonians passage. "Why do preachers and Christian movies use the theme 'thief in the night' to teach a 'surprise' Rapture, when I Thessalonians 5:4 says believers will not be surprised?"

He studied the section a moment and then replied, "I don't know." Although this author refers to I Thessalonians 5:4 in a book he wrote, he prefaces it's use with, "We don't know when the Rapture will occur...but according to the signs, we are in the general time."

This encounter was significant because of this man's extensive studies of the end times. It was mystifying. Why have we all, including that dedicated prophetic teacher, applied the passage this way? This question led me to investigate further.

Interestingly, I found most scholars believe the passage in I Thessalonians, chapter 5 is not a direct reference to the Rapture. They reach this conclusion because of the specific term, "the day of the Lord."[92] They feel the use of the phrase, "the day of the Lord" describes either (a) the whole seven-year period of judgment on the earth (along with the simultaneous seven-year preparation of the Bride in heaven); (b) the period from the Rapture to the end of the Millennium; or (c) the climactic end of the seven-year Tribulation.[a]

One truth however, can be agreed upon here. This passage does teach that this appearance of Jesus will come as unexpectedly as a thief—**to unbelievers.**[b][93]

Most importantly though, **this particular passage** does not teach that **Christians** cannot know the timing of future events! Based on this discovery, I decided then to reexamine the other Scriptures that prohibit exact dating of end-time events.

---

[a] Note Revelation 16:15, which is a definite reference to the second coming of Jesus, uses the same terminology, "I come as a thief." The thief analogy also used in the Olivet discourse will be demonstrated in the next chapter to be another reference to the Second Coming of Jesus. See also Day of The Lord passages, Isaiah 13:6-10; Jeremiah 30:4-8; Zephaniah 1:14-23.

[b] A thoughtful study of all fifteen occurrences of "thief" in the New Testament produces an interesting profile. It seems every use of this word is in the negative. *See* endnote for further discussion.

CHAPTER 11
WHAT WE CANNOT KNOW

The scriptural objection most often voiced to dating the Rapture is, "But the Bible says 'no man knows the day and the hour.'" Trying to compute these dates would certainly be futile:

> (A) if these words from Jesus' speech to His disciples given on the Mount of Olives refer to the Rapture, and
> (B) if they tell us **no one** could **ever** know exact dates of end-time events.

However, in studying the two occurrences of these words some surprising points emerged.

The first question that must be addressed is, "What 'hour' is being referred to in this statement? In this chapter we will seek specifically to discover if these words from the Olivet discourse refer to the Rapture.

It is essential to notice that both occurrences of "No man knoweth the day or the hour" are **preceded** by these statements:

> 1. Matthew 24:29, "*Immediately after the tribulation... Son of man coming in the clouds of heaven...*(verse 30) *all these things be fulfilled* (verse 34)."

2. Mark 13:26 (after Jesus describes the awfulness of the Tribulation), "*then shall they see the Son of man coming in the clouds with great power and glory.*"

Notice also the companion passage in Luke 21:27, 31, (which records the same speech given in Matthew and Mark):
1. "*And then shall they see the Son of man coming in a cloud with power and great glory. So likewise ye, when ye see these things come to pass know ye that the Kingdom of God is nigh.*" (Note "after" and "and then" **follows** the description of the seven, long, painful years of tribulation.)

2. Notice the three previous Scriptures say, "*They shall see the Son of man coming in great power and glory.*" This information becomes vital since (by definition of the Rapture) Jesus is seen by everyone **only at His Second Coming.**

3. Jesus foretold in Luke 17:22–37 (after giving the analogies of the rescues of Noah and Lot), "*Even thus shall it be in the day when the Son of man is revealed.*" The revealing of the Son of man can only be the Second Coming, since Jesus is **not revealed** in the Rapture.

After looking at all three instances of this discourse in the Gospels, it appears that Jesus is teaching about His Second Coming and the end of the great Tribulation, not the Rapture.

Many Agree

It has been of particular interest to me to note the number of solid Bible teachers who have expressed this same viewpoint regarding these passages. Following are the statements of just four of them:

1. Harry A. Ironside states in his book *Matthew*, with regard to chapter 24, "The secret of the Rapture of the Church, prior to the end-time is not introduced here in this great prophetic discourse. That was still a hidden mystery when Jesus spoke these words." Referring to finding the Rapture in Matthew, chapter 24 he continues. "There is no time set for it, nor are there any signs indicated. The signs here all have to do with His revelation from heaven as the King who is to return to take His great power and reign. The coming of the Son of man refers always to this event, **never to the Rapture!**"[a][94]

2. Arno C. Gaebelein writes concerning Matthew 24, in his book, *The Gospel of Matthew*, "We say once more that this has nothing to do with the Church. The removal of the Church takes place before the last day of Daniel's prophecy begins and when the Lord comes immediately after the days of tribulation, the Church is with Him and in His Glory the Church is manifested. The revelation concerning His coming for the Church is recorded in I Thessalonians 4:15–18. To make the elect in Matthew 24:30 the Church, as it is done so often, is **bewildering and a wrong interpretation.**[b] This part of the Olivet discourse, as we have shown, has nothing whatever to do with the Church."[95]

3. John Walvoord teaches in *Matthew—Thy Kingdom Come*, "Those who believe that the Rapture, or translation of the Church, occurs before the time of trouble at the end of the age, usually do not believe the Rapture is in view at all

---

[a] Emphasis mine.

[b] Emphasis mine.

in this discourse, as the Rapture was first introduced in John 14:1–3, sometime after the Olivet discourse...If the details of this discourse are observed and interpreted literally, it fits best with the view that the Rapture is not revealed in this discourse at all, but is a later revelation, introduced by Christ in John 14 and revealed in more detail in I Corinthians 15 and I Thessalonians 4.

"The entire passage from Matthew 24:15–31 is the specific answer to the disciples of the sign of His coming and of the end of the age, with the climactic sign being the Second Coming and the glory that attends it, and will fulfill the prophecy of Acts 1:11 that Christ will return as He went up into heaven, that is His return will be physical, gradual, visible, and with clouds. Matthew 24:31 brings to a close the first doctrinal section of the Olivet discourse, and what follows is a series of applications and illustrations.

"In interpreting the illustrations which follow, while there may be secondary applications of the truth to the Church awaiting the Rapture, **the laws of exegesis[c] would dictate that the illustrations should relate to the doctrine of the Second Coming of Christ.**"[96d]

4. Referring to Matthew 24:40, 41 J. Vernon McGee remarks in *Matthew*, "I can hear someone saying to me, 'Well preacher, you have finally painted yourself into a corner. You said **the Church and the Rapture are not in the Olivet discourse[e]** and here they are. Two shall be in the field and one shall be taken and the other shall be left.'" McGee

---

[c] A critical explanation of a portion of Scriptures.

[d] Emphasis mine.

[e] Emphasis mine.

repeats, **"This is not a reference to the Rapture of the Church."**[97] [f]

Again and again I've heard noted radio Bible teachers say, "We used to believe these Scriptures in the Olivet discourse were referring to the Rapture, but we see now that this is a section on the Second Coming of Jesus."

This knowledge alone should caution us not to use Matthew 24:36 or Mark 13:32 as proof texts that no one can "know the day or the hour" of the **Rapture.**

Does Noah "Sink" This Premise?

Some hold to the thought that the "coming" spoken of in Matthew, chapter 24 must be the Rapture because of the reference to Noah's time. Verses 37−39 say, *"But as the days of Noe[g] were, so shall also the coming of the Son of man be. For as in the days that were before the flood they were eating and drinking, marrying and giving in marriage, until the day that Noe entered into the ark, and knew not until the flood came, and took them all away; so shall the coming of the Son of man be."*

They say, "The comparison made here by Jesus is that Noah's time was the same as the time before the Rapture. People in Noah's day are described as eating, drinking and marrying, living life as usual." They explain, "It has to be the Rapture since the Second Coming described in Revelation is at the end of the Tribulation and since that time will be so terrible, as God rains down successive judgments from heaven, in no way could you describe it as 'life as usual.'"

In answer to this thought, I'd like to suggest that "life as usual" can have several meanings. First of all, let's take a close look at the people who were destroyed in both the flood and Sodom and Gomorrah.

---

[f] Emphasis mine.

[g] New Testament spelling of Noah.

In Noah's day we see rampant sin and disregard for any of God's restraints. God's description of the antediluvian[h] population just before the flood paints a desperately evil time. Granted, it was not a time exactly like the end of the Tribulation will be, but it had to be somewhat similar. People running amuck without any godly restraint, had created a world problem so bad that the Bible states that *"it repented the Lord that He had made man on the earth."* In fact God describes seeing *"that the wickedness of man was great in the earth, and that every imagination of the thoughts of his heart was only evil continually."*[i]

That life goes on without any thought for the God who created them, is what I believe this New Testament Scripture is emphasizing.

The "life being lived as if God didn't exist" interpretation of this passage as well as "life as usual" holds true in Lot's example, also. Life just before the destruction of Sodom and Gomorrah could hardly be described as normal. Men in Sodom were so taken in the depravity of homosexuality that even being struck blind by God did not deter them from trying to pollute the bodies of the "new men in town."[j] Indeed, the "life as usual" pictured in the time before the flood and the population destroyed in Lot's day certainly are not "pastoral pictures."

The Bible describes the last days as "perilous times,"[k] yet, in a sense, life does go on even during the Tribulation. God says there will be buying and selling.[l] In fact, just

---

[h] Those living before the flood.

[i] Genesis 6:5, 6

[j] Genesis 19:1-11

[k] II Timothy 3:1-7

[l] Revelation 13:16, 17

before Jesus' Second Coming described in Revelation, chapter 19, we see mention of kings, merchants, rich men, shipmasters, and sailors, as well as great cities, wealth, slavery, musicians, craftsmen, bridegrooms, brides, and nations.[m] All these indicate that even though the judgments from God devastate both mankind and our planet, man continues to carry on his earthly activities.[n]

Timing of Noah and the Flood

Another piece of information that bolsters the Second Coming view of Matthew 24 is the sequence of events in Genesis when Noah entered the ark. A close study of Genesis chapter 7, particularly verses 2–4, 7, 8, 10, and 16) shows us that, 1) Noah and his family boarded the ark, 2) the animals went in, 3) God shut the door, 4) everyone inside waited seven days, 5) the rain began, and 6) all air-breathing antediluvian life not on the ark drowned.

The verses supporting this viewpoint of flood events are thirteen and fourteen which clarify that people and animals all entered the ark on the same day; verse seven which says Noah and company went in; and verse ten which informs us, "...and it came to pass after seven days, that the waters of the flood were upon the earth." If this suggested scenario is correct, then Matthew 24:37–39 shows us in (type) the destruction of antediluvian society being compared to the destruction of the Tribulation population.

Some still may feel the Rapture must be contained inside the Olivet discourse because the population in Noah's day is described as enjoying life. Those who perceive the horrible time at the end of the Tribulation to be just too

---

[m] Revelation 18:9-24

[n] Compare the Egyptian society (government and military) continuing even after a succession of devastating disasters. Exodus 7-14.

terrible to be described as "life as usual" must consider the impact of the timing of Noah's rescue.

We cannot discount the important interval of time between Noah's rescue and the actual destruction of the flood. *"Until the day that Noah entered into the ark, and knew not until [seven days later] the flood came and took them all away."*[o] Again, even though the pre-flood populace was described in Noah's day to be thoroughly rotten, they still had the seven days to encounter changes while Noah rested safely in the ark. These seven days could easily typify the hard times of the Tribulation.

The Reason for Reference to Noah's Day

It seems more likely that Jesus' comparison of Noah's and Lot's generations to the future unbelieving generation concerns their **"know-not"** status.

We know by reading II Peter 2:5 that the population in Noah's day heard about the impending judgment, but did not believe the warning. *"And spared not the old world, but saved Noah the eighth person, a preacher of righteousness, bringing in the flood upon the world of the ungodly."* This attitude of unbelief is repeated in the behavior of the people living during the Tribulation as they will choose to blaspheme God rather than repent and be saved. They actually do not believe God will ultimately judge them. In rebellion, they go out to war against Him.

Revelation says, *"They repented not of their deeds,"* and *"I saw the beast and, the kings of the earth, and their armies, gathered together to make war against him that sat on the horse, and against his army."*[p]

---

[o] Matthew 24:38, 39

[p] Revelation 16:11, 19:19

We also see this determined attitude of unbelief in II Peter 3:3—7, *"Knowing this first, that there shall come in the last days scoffers walking after their own lust;*

And saying, Where is the promise of his coming? for since the fathers fell asleep, all things continue as they were from the beginning of the creation.

For this they willingly are ignorant of, that by the word of God the heavens were of old, and the earth standing out of the water and in the water:

Whereby the world that then was, being overflowed with water, perished:

But the heavens and the earth, which are now, by the same word are kept in store, reserved unto fire against the day of judgment and perdition of ungodly men."

I believe the Matthew 24 passage teaches that **life was as usual** *"until the day that Noe entered the ark."* Then, referring to the population shut outside of the ark, they *"knew not until the flood came and took them all away."* They "knew not" what? They "knew not" that they were going to be destroyed by God! The same attitude of disbelief concerning impending destruction will exist before the Second Coming of Christ. The scoffing generation of II Peter 3:3—7 that will receive the seven years of Revelation judgment from God, is said to be *"willingly ignorant"* of the impending judgment.

The rest of chapter 24 and the whole of chapter 25 continues to contrast those who know and expect Jesus' return with those who don't care and postpone getting right with God, thus receiving judgment.

The story of Noah is such a beautiful picture of the preservation of believers. Throughout Noah's life, God gave successively more detailed information about the impending judgment and God's promised rescue of Noah and his family. This information is listed in Genesis chapters 5—8.

Information first came through the name Enoch gave to his son. This name "Methuselah" means, "When he is

gone it will come." The flood actually came the year that
Methuselah died! Then God gave the promise of 120 years
yet to come. Next, God sent the animals to Noah, told him
to load the food supply and last He gave the invitation to
step aboard. Noah was also given the **exact time** of the
judgment of the earth in Genesis 7:7, *"For yet seven days and I
will cause it to rain upon the earth."*[q]

This principle, of God **telling believers** shortly before
He rescues them from the judgment of unbelievers, is
suggested in Amos 3:7. *"Surely the Lord God will do nothing,
but he revealeth his secret unto his servants the prophets."*[r]

We see this again, demonstrated in God's foretelling
Abraham about His plan to destroy Sodom and Gomorrah.[s]
After informing Abraham, God sent angels **to warn Lot**
about the impending destruction. These angels advised Lot,
*"Whatsoever thou hast in the city, bring them out of this place: For
we will destroy this place."* Lot quickly informed his family
about imminent doom. His sons-in-law discounted the
whole story as a big joke choosing not to believe a word Lot
said.

The next morning the angels hurried Lot and his
three family members who did believe the warning, out of
the city. *"Then the Lord rained upon Sodom and upon Gomorrah
brimstone and fire from the Lord out of heaven."* The sons-in-law
died.[t]

---

[q] A possible allusion to the Rapture in this whole flood scenario is that Noah represents the raptured believers. This is seen in the fact that seven days before the total judgment upon mankind, the Lord called Noah into the ark and the Lord shut the door. Genesis 7:1,4,16.

[r] Although some teachers maintain that this Scripture only applies to the prophets of God who recorded God's messages in the Bible, the ultimate conclusion remains the same. God through His word (via human scribes) gives believers information concerning the future (including impending judgments).

[s] Genesis 18:17-33

[t] Genesis 19:14-16

Again, we see progressive understanding[u] given to believers concerning their rescue from the impending judgment coming against unbelievers.

The comparison of the unaware, uncaring, unbelieving population who lived in the city of Sodom just before it was destroyed by God to the population that is judged by God at the end of the Tribulation is made by Jesus in Luke 17:28–30. *"Likewise also as it was in the days of Lot; they did eat, they drank, they bought, they sold, they planted, they builded;*

But the same day that Lot went out of Sodom it rained fire and brimstone from heaven and destroyed them all.

Even thus shall it be in the day when the Son of man is revealed."[v]

This principle of **telling believers ahead of time** about being rescued from impending destruction is summed up by Jesus.[w] After telling the disciples what would transpire during the seven-year Tribulation, He summed up how believers should respond to this awesome information. *"And when these things begin to come to pass, then look up, and lift up your heads; for your redemption draweth nigh."*

One Taken—One Left

Some Bible expositors see the Rapture in Matthew 24 for a different reason. They hold the thought that the latter part of the Olivet discourse of Jesus in Matthew 24:40–51 (repeated in Luke 17:30–37), is a definite picture of the Rapture of the believers. Calling this "the Rapture section" is

---

[u] Since the completion of the Scriptures in A.D. 90 , "new" information comes from a clearer and deeper understanding of the Bible.

[v] Note this depiction, "the Son of man revealed," is a description of the bodily, visible second coming of Jesus not the call of Jesus for believers called the Rapture.

[w] Luke 21:28

based on the "*one taken—one left*" illustrations of Matthew 24:40 and 41.

This conclusion is based on the Greek word "airo" which is "to lift, to take up or away" translated into English "took" in Matthew 24:39. "*And knew not until the flood took them all away.*" This "took" is about the populace who died in the flood and is an obvious reference to judgment.

Next it is pointed out that the word "taken" as used in the following verses is the Greek word "paralambano" which means "to receive near, to associate with oneself." They insist that the word "paralambano" is **always and only** used in a positive or friendly sense.

"*Then shall two be in the field; the one shall be taken, and the other left.*

Two women shall be grinding at the mill; the one shall be taken, and the other left."

They say these people are taken up with Jesus. They do not see the "taken ones" as going into Judgment (which would make it a Second Coming passage).

Since "paralambano" is formed by combining "para" (meaning "near" or "beside") with "lambano" (meaning "to take"), they conclude that the compound word produced could not be used to describe people being taken away in judgment.

It is then expertly pointed out that this **same word, "paralambano"** is translated into English in John 14:3 as "receive." The importance of this, they say, is that, "the word paralambano is selected by Jesus to describe taking the Church to Himself, just as He used it earlier in Matthew 24."

Judgment or Heaven

At first sight this viewpoint is convincing. However, a study of **every** use of the Greek word "paralambano" in the Bible reveals an interesting insight. Paralambano is used forty-eight times in the New Testament. Interestingly, fourteen uses of it describe the taker or the destination as **negative**. Examples of this use are, "*Then the devil taketh him,*" "*Then goeth he, and taketh with himself seven other spirits more wicked than himself.*" and "*They took Jesus and led him away.*"[x]

John F. Walvrood comments about the premise that "paralambano" is always used in a friendly sense in *The Rapture Question*. He states this premise "is destroyed by the fact that the same word is used in John 19:16−17 in reference to taking Jesus to the cross, an obvious act of judgment which contradicts the statement that the word is always used in a friendly sense."[98]

The conclusion that the people in Matthew 24:40, 41 are taken into judgment seems to fit the context of the passage best. The last two verses of this chapter describe the **punishment** of those who are not ready when the lord of the servant returns. "*The lord of that servant shall come in a day when he looketh not for him, and in an hour that he is not aware of, and shall cut him asunder, and appoint him his portion with the hypocrites; there shall be weeping and gnashing of teeth.*"[y]

The passage in Luke is even more direct in explaining that the people who are "taken" in the Olivet discourse are taken to judgment. "*I tell you, in that night there shall be two men in one bed; the one shall be taken, and the other shall be left.*

Two women shall be grinding together; the one shall be taken, and the other shall be left.

Two men shall be in the field; the one shall be taken, and the other shall be left.

And they answered and said unto him, Where Lord? And he said unto them, whithersoever the body is, thither will the eagles be gathered together."[z] Based on the symbolism throughout

---

[x] Matthew 4:5, 12:45; John 19:26

[y] Matthew 24: 50, 51

[z] Luke 17:34-37

the Bible of eagles gathering to devour dead bodies, this surely sounds like judgment!^{aa}

Compare Jesus' answer in Luke, to the Second Coming judgment. *"And he cried with a loud voice, saying to all the fowls that fly in the midst of heaven, Come and gather yourselves unto the supper of the great God; That ye may eat the flesh of kings...of captains...of mighty men...of horses...of them that sit on them...of all men free and bond, both great and small."*^{bb}

One more difficulty of calling the "one taken—one left" section of Luke 17:36—36 a "Rapture section" is found in verse thirty. It precedes the "one taken—one left" passage and states: *"Thus shall it be in the last day when the Son of man is revealed."* This has to be the time at the end of the seven-year Tribulation when *"every eye shall see"* Jesus coming back in His glorious Second Coming.

The "one taken" of the Olivet discourse must of necessity be those living on earth who have taken the mark of the beast, as well as those who have refused to believe that Jesus was ever coming back. These will be taken away into judgment. They will not be left with the believing remnant who will populate the earth during Jesus' millennial reign of peace.^{cc}

Indeed, it appears most likely that Jesus' words, "No man knoweth the day or the hour" is a reference to His Second Coming, **not to the Rapture.**^{dd}

---

^{aa} Job 39:27-30; Matthew 24:28

^{bb} Revelation 19:17, 18

^{cc} Revelation 1:7, 19:17-21

^{dd} How amazing to observe the countless teachers and preachers who definitely believe that the Rapture is not contained in the Olivet discourse, yet, they still continue to pull out the one verse "No man knows the day nor the hour" as a prooftext for not being able to know the date of the Rapture!

CHAPTER 12
CAN'T KNOW NOW OR EVER

Some will quickly note, "Well if this 'day and hour' that we can't know is the Second Coming, it doesn't work scripturally! If we could know the exact Rapture date, we could determine the exact day of the Second Coming right now. We could simply add the seven years of Tribulation to discover the date that Jesus said no one could know!

Yes, that would be true, except for two reasons.

First, do we have an abundance of Scriptures that prove that the countdown for the seven years of Tribulation begins at the exact moment of the Rapture?

Second, even if we couldn't know the day of the Rapture, anyone living during the seven-year Tribulation could count 1,260 days from the "abomination" spoken of in Daniel, chapter 9 and Revelation, chapter 12 to discover the **exact day** of the Second Coming. These people would then know what the Bible says they can't know!

That puts a real twist in our interpretation of what we can and cannot know.

A Reasonable Answer

As we ponder this question let us also review the second part of the original question in chapter 11, (B) Does Jesus tell us in the Olivet discourse that **no one but God would ever know** the exact day and hour of the Rapture and of the Second Coming? This is a **vital factor** to consider before we can comfortably use these passages to rule out ever knowing a specific Rapture date.

The twenty-fourth chapter of Matthew begins with the disciples questioning Jesus. *"Tell us, when shall these things be? and what shall be the sign of thy coming, and of the end of the world?"*

Jesus doesn't answer their questions immediately, but instead He describes many awesome events that would occur before His coming and the end of the world. His discourse begins in verse four and continues through verse thirty-five. Only then does Jesus finally answer the disciple's original question. He states; *"But of that day and hour knoweth no man, no, not the angels in heaven."* Notice the exact information given to His disciples. It is: Neither angels nor men knew the day of his coming.

Consider Jesus

While we consider the accuracy of this observation, look at the parallel passage in Mark 13:32, *"But of that day and that hour knoweth no man, no, not the angels which are in heaven, neither the Son, but the father."* Note here that not only angels and men are listed as not knowing the date of the Second Coming of Jesus, but the **Son** also names Himself as not knowing! This piece of information makes the whole search very intriguing.

If we decide that these two passages teach that no person could **ever** know the day and hour of the Second Coming, then we would also have to conclude that Jesus would not know the date of His departure for the Rapture until it's exact moment!

We need to take a moment to consider how the Son of God, Jesus, very God Himself, could **ever** not know anything.

Many Bible scholars feel that from the time Jesus was born of a virgin, walked the earth, was tempted, died, was resurrected, and once again ascended to the Father, He chose to set aside and not use His powers of the Godhead. They believe Jesus willingly elected not to exercise His powers of omnipresence, omnipotence, and omniscience, even though He still was God.

J. Vernon McGee comments on this verse in *Mark*. "This verse is admittedly difficult. If Jesus is God, it is difficult to account for this lack of omniscience. *'Neither the Son'* is added by Mark (Compare Matthew 24:36). Mark presents Jesus as *'the servant, and the servant knoweth not what his Lord doeth.'* The servant character of Jesus represents His most typical and true humanity. He *'took on the form of a servant.'* When He became a man, He limited Himself in order to be made like us. He **was not omnipresent when He became man.**"[99]

There are other examples of Scriptures that lead to this belief. Luke 2:52 states, *"Jesus increased in wisdom."* This infers that Jesus had to study just as we do. Of course the meaning of Hebrews 4:15, *"but was in all points tempted like as we are,"* becomes a greater reality to us knowing that Jesus must have been tempted not to persevere in scriptural studies much as we are tempted.

This "setting aside" of godly attributes is further deduced from Jesus' potential to be tempted, His need to be ministered to, His increase in strength of spirit, His need for food, His calling upon God for miracles, His thirst, and His being fashioned as a man.[a]

---

[a] Matthew 4:1, 2, 11; Luke 2:40, 52, 24:41-43; John 11:41, 42, 19:28; Philippians 2:5-8

Scripture makes clear the depth of commitment the very God, Jesus, made to come live, die, and rise again in order to provide salvation for us. *"For verily he took not on him the nature of angels; but he took on him the nature of Abraham. Wherefore in all things it behoved him to be made like unto his brethren, that he might be a merciful and faithful high priest in things pertaining to God, to make reconciliation for the sins of the people."[b]*

One of the passages previously mentioned that indicates this voluntary setting aside of godly capabilities, actually concerns prophetic dates.[c] Jesus explained, *"...knoweth no man...neither the son."* This statement of Jesus conclusively proves that He did not know everything **(at least when He spoke these words)**. This verse also seems to infer that He was not using His omniscience as He spoke to His disciples. Since the Bible is very clear that Jesus is God, then the only way He could not have *"known the day or the hour"* as He spoke was, as Philippians 2:5–8 states, because of His voluntary, temporary, submission to live in the humble form of a human.

Most importantly, note Jesus's answer in Mark to the disciples' question of, *"When shall these things be?"* He answers, *"Of that day and hour knoweth no man, no, not the angels which are in heaven, neither the Son, but the Father."* He does **not** say, "I will **never** know the day nor hour, neither will any man."

Concluding that Jesus would never know the day or hour until the moment of departure in order to hold on to the "it's impossible to date idea," presents an impossible problem. Even if Jesus were not to be told His departure date until it arrived, He could calculate it quite easily when He saw the abomination of desolation occur. He would

[b] Hebrews 2:16-18

[c] Mark 13:32

need only to apply His knowledge of the Scripture in Daniel and Revelation and calculate the number of days from the abomination.

This biblical date setting, using the information from Daniel, could also be done by the 144,000 Jews who are sealed during the seven-year Tribulation. In fact, during the Tribulation, anyone who looked into the prophecies of Daniel could calculate **the exact day** of Jesus' Second Coming!

Serious students of prophecy, who hold the belief, "You can know the general time and the seasons of the Rapture but definitely not the day and the hour," must consider yet another Scripture.

Just before Jesus was taken up into heaven, His disciples asked, *"Wilt thou at this time restore again the kingdom to Israel?"* Oh no! Here the disciples go again, asking Jesus to give them the time of Israel's kingdom age. Please, note carefully every word of Jesus' reply to them. *"And He said unto them, 'It is not for you to know the times or the seasons, which the Father hath put in his own power."* It's interesting to note that according to *Strong's Exhaustive Concordance* the word "time" in this verse come from the Greek root word "kairos" which means "set or proper time" while the word translated "seasons" comes from the Greek word "chronos" which means "a space of time." The translators saw a difference in the meaning of the two words as they are used in this verse. "Time" refers to an **occasion** and "seasons" is a specific (but larger) **expanse of time.** In the same way the word "chronos" is used in Acts 14:17 and translated fruitful "seasons."

Do you see the problem that this verse presents? We are informed from Scriptures[d] about the kind of conditions

---

[d] II Timothy 3:1-5

that will exist in the last days. This means that the **general time of the end can be known** by believers, yet Acts 1:7 says the **times and the seasons cannot be known!** Could it be, as previously discussed, that the prohibition to know the exact hour of end-time occurrences applied only to believers of Jesus' day?

Considering all of the preceding information, it appears the solid information that we derive from "*no man knoweth the day or the hour*" is that A) Jesus is referring to the Second Coming **not the Rapture** and B) **only at the time Jesus spoke these words** was the date known exclusively by God the Father.

CHAPTER 13
THE PURPOSE OF IMMINENCE

At this point many Christians quickly speak up and say, "The imminence of Christ's return has always been a strong motivating factor in the history of the Christian church."

That is most certainly true. From the days of the apostles until this very day, imminence has been an integral part of our Christian experience. However, when some go on to suggest that, "If believers were to know the exact date of the Rapture, they would go out and live in wild sin until just before Jesus' coming," I most heartily disagree. Could anyone really believe that the only reason Christians live their lives honoring the Lord is because they are afraid to get caught sinning when the Rapture comes? This running-out-to-sin objection, gives the impression that all believers constantly crave a life of wickedness, and that the Christian life of obedience is without present reward of joy.

Certainly, at times, the thought of the imminent return of Christ spurs us on, but for the most part our obedience is a result of a desire to please the Lord. The thought of imminence, as it has traditionally been interpreted from Scripture, is definitely motivational. However, if we were to discover that the exact date of the Rapture was to occur in the time we were living, that knowledge would be the biggest spur for service yet!

Another thought of some is, "To deny imminence is to take the hope of His coming away from every previous generation." In considering this idea, one needs to review God's promise (Genesis, chapter 3) of a coming redeemer to be born of a woman.

Many theologians discuss women's belief in the imminent arrival of the redeemer man-child when they teach Genesis, chapter 4.[a] Donald Barnhouse, in *Genesis*, explains that Eve's statement at Cain's birth shows her belief that this child was the promised Messiah. "In Hebrew the true meaning is found. 'I have gotten a man, even the deliverer.'"[100]

As God gave the added promise that this redeemer would come from the womb of a Jewish mother, the conviction of imminence continued among Jewish women. Even though the Lord began to weave into the Old Testament Scriptures (particularly the book of Daniel) some details as to when this man-child Messiah would come upon the scene, Jewish mothers continued to hope that they might be the chosen vessel. The motivating promise of the imminent arrival of the Messiah was every bit real to them, even though with hindsight we can look back today and know that Messiah would not arrive until thousands of years after the original promise.

In the same way believers of past generations who have looked for the promised Rapture in their lifetimes have been motivated by the possibility of His coming. That some future generation (perhaps ours) might actually know the time of the Rapture can in no way take away the hope of these previous generations of believers.

---

[a] *See* McGee's, *Genesis*, as well as John J. Davis', *Paradise to Prison*.

The Doctrine of Imminence

In examining the widely-held and most-revered
doctrine of imminence, some interesting information
surfaces. Two proofs are said to carry this doctrine:
1. The early church held the doctrine of imminence and,
2. the Scriptures teach it.

Concerning the first point, I certainly agree that most
believers throughout history have lived with expectancy.
But we must also remember that for at least four thousand
years mankind lived with another promised hope. They
looked for a man born of woman who would defeat Satan.
Of course, the Jews (in particular) lived with the imminent
hope of the coming Messiah for nearly two thousand years.
However, throughout that whole era of expectancy, God
gave successive bits of information as to when this Messiah
would arrive.

From this example we see that **until or unless we
receive definite information about the time of any coming
event, we live in expectancy.** However, this truth does not
preclude the possibility of ever comprehending more of the
information (we already have) about specific timing.

Now let us scrutinize the second reason given for the
doctrine of imminence.

After examining all the Scriptures garnered by the
most ardent exponents of imminence, one truth becomes
evident. All of the Scriptures given concern expectation, and
promise, for the purpose of exhortation and encouragement.[b]
None of these "imminence" verses refer one way or another
to knowledge about when the Rapture may occur.

For example, the description of the Rapture in I
Corinthians 15:51 stating that we are raised "*in the twinkling*

---

[b] John 14:2-3; Acts 1:11; I Corinthians 1:7, 15:51-52; Philippians 3:20-21; Colossians 3:4; I
Thessalonians 1:9-10, 4:16-17, 5:5-9; I Timothy 6:14; Titus 2:13; James 5:8-9; I Peter 3:3-4;
Revelation 3:10, 22:17-22

of an eye" is used by many teachers to prove imminence. In actuality, this "twinkling of an eye" simply describes the instantaneous nature of the occurrence. Many happenings in life are quick, such as the striking of a match, or the blaze of a flashbulb. Just because an incident is quick, does not necessarily mean it is unknown ahead of time.

Let me give a hometown example of imminence. If I drive over and drop my daughter off at a friend's house to play, I might say, "Honey, I'm going to run some errands and then swing back to pick you up. You be good now!" She knows I'm coming back, that I'll pick her up in the car, and that she should behave.

Now I may come back in a few minutes or a few hours. I may just drive up without warning or I might call her from my last stop and tell her, "I'll be by to pick you up in five minutes."

In the same way, when you examine each of the "imminence" verses you'll see the type of information given to us by God concerning the Rapture is similar to what I gave to my daughter about picking her up.

None of **these** verses state that the time could never be known. Until or unless believers receive details about the time of the Rapture, we live just knowing, "He's coming, maybe today." The expectancy taught in these verses in no way precludes the possibility of **ever** knowing an exact date for the Rapture.

It's astonishing to me that there are so many theologians who on the one hand adamantly teach that "there are no signs which must precede the Rapture" while at the same time they give stirring sermons saying, "Just look at the signs. We are in the last days!"

I agree that we should look for Jesus, not just signs that precede Him. That is exactly what this whole book is intended to do! It should encourage believers to actively look for the time of our departure to be with Jesus.

Since in the previous chapters the "prohibition" verses are seen mostly to be references to the Second Coming which in reality only to apply to the believers of Jesus day, it seems time that the body of Christ rethink its traditional stand on the dating of end-time occurrences.

Not Always Imminent

The belief from the very beginning of the birth of the Church was, "Jesus could come back at any time." Since the early church knew only that they were to be ready and that Jesus would come back, the climate of expectancy existed. But the added idea that "There has never been any circumstance or happening that needs to occur before the Rapture could transpire" must be examined.

In considering this thought, God's Word, not the longevity of a belief must be our guide. Upon examination of the following Scriptures, perhaps this belief needs to be redefined.

1. It is commonly understood that Jesus told Peter the type of death he would experience.[c] Although there is a difference of opinion as to whether the death Jesus foretold was martyrdom or old age, the importance of this encounter to prophetic study is that **as long as Peter was alive, the Rapture could not occur!** The fact that Peter would **die** (and therefore not be raptured) is also mentioned by Peter long after the encounter recorded in the book of John.[d]

According to this information, imminence was not in effect, at least until Peter's death. This passage then contradicts the often repeated statement that "There is not,

---

[c] John 21:18-23

[d] II Peter 1:14

nor has there ever been anything that must occur before the Rapture."

2. **The Lord specifically speaks of Paul's future on earth.** Three days after Paul's conversion, God reveals that Paul will "*bear my name before the Gentiles, and kings, and the children of Israel: For I will shew him how great things he must suffer for my name's sake.*"[e] Again the idea that the Rapture always could have occurred at any time fails in the light of God's words. The Rapture could not have happened until Paul witnessed to the Gentiles, kings, and the Jews, nor until Paul had "suffered great things." Since Jesus promised to take all the believers in the Rapture, including Paul, it simply could not occur until Paul fulfilled God's prophecy.

Watchfulness Encouraged

We are all familiar with the statement of Jesus, "*Therefore be ye also ready, for in such an hour as ye think not the Son of man cometh.*"[f] Should we conclude from this statement that no Christian will ever know the time of the Rapture?

To answer this question please note that the people being reprimanded in this passage are **the ones who did not watch, and were therefore "surprised" at His arrival.** Besides, isn't this passage, as previously discussed, a discourse about the timing of **the Second Coming of Jesus, not the Rapture?**

Why, do we continue to use this verse as a reason that the exact moment of the Rapture cannot be known? Could the reason for the constant misapplication of Second Coming verses to the Rapture be because this belief has a weak base?

---

[e] Acts 9:15, 16

[f] Matthew 24:42, 44

There are three groups of "watch" verses that pertain to end-time events. The first group relates to watchfulness during the Tribulation to avoid judgment. These Scriptures,[g] mostly from the Olivet discourse, are seen by many such as McGee, Walvrood, and the contributors to *The Pulpit Commentary*, to be definite references to the Second Coming.[101]

The second group of "watch" or "look" verses[h] tells us as New Testament believers to watch (or monitor) our conduct.

Just a few of all the "watch" and "look" verses[i] might be referring to the Rapture (as opposed to the Second Coming). If these verses refer to the Rapture, are we to believe that God is telling us to tilt our heads back so we can see Jesus when He comes for us, or is He suggesting that we be in a ready condition of holy living? Is He not also exhorting us to study and correctly interpret the Scriptures so that we will be aware of the time of His coming?

No matter which of these ideas we choose, we know that those who "watch" **will not be surprised when Jesus comes!** This conclusion is strongly borne out in the Bible, *"Be watchful, and strengthen the things which remain, that are ready to die; for I have not found thy works perfect before God. Remember therefore how thou hast received and heard, and hold fast, and repent. if therefore thou shalt not watch, I will come on thee as a thief, and thou shalt not know what hour I will come upon thee."*[j]

---

[g] Matthew 24:42-25:13; Mark 13:33-37; Luke 21:35-36 and Hebrews 9:28

[h] I Corinthians 16:13; Colossians 4:2 and II Timothy 4:5

[i] I Thessalonians 5:6; Titus 2:13 and I Peter 4:7

[j] Revelation 3:2, 3

CHAPTER 14
HIDDEN INFORMATION

The logical thought occurring in most Christian's minds at this point is, "If the application of these Scripture passages with regard to specific Rapture dating is correct, then why haven't any theologians throughout the centuries discovered this interpretation?"

This question is indeed appropriate when one considers the universality of the historic misapplication of the Rapture to both I Thessalonians, chapter 5 and Matthew, chapter 24.

Could the reason for this strange, two-thousand-year-old misunderstanding be a demonstration of the perfect timing of God? Might He have closed our discernment of some verses and allowed a misunderstanding to exist among Christians for almost two thousand years?

This principle of withholding understanding is used in Daniel 12:4, 8 and 9. *"But thou, O Daniel, shut up the words, and seal the book, even to the time of the end...And I heard, but I understood not: then said I, O my Lord, what shall be the end of these things? And he said, Go thy way, Daniel: for the words are closed up and sealed till the time of the end."*[102]

Note that even though Jesus told his disciples that the Holy Spirit would *"guide you into all truth"* and that *"He will show you things to come,"*[a] the men who heard these words did

---

[a] John 16:13

not necessarily comprehend everything they heard or even wrote. John, who recorded this promise of the coming Spirit, also observed the Revelation of Jesus Christ. Jesus in this Revelation instructed John simply to record what he saw. There is no indication that John, nor the prophetic writers of the Old Testament, actually understood all the fulfillments or timing of the visions given to them by God.

It is consistent with God's other dealings with mankind to seal up the information in Daniel (and other end time prophecies) until He is ready to reveal it to His children. Note how Paul prefaced his words revealing the Rapture, *"Behold I shew you a mystery."*[b] This indicates the unveiling of a truth not previously revealed to, or understood by mankind. Through Paul, God then proclaims a beautiful promise to believers of the newly initiated Church age. *"We shall not all sleep, but we shall all be changed, In a moment in the twinkling of an eye, at the last trump: for the dead shall be raised incorruptible, and we shall all be changed."*

If God had allowed us to decipher the exact dates long before the actual time of the end, then the admonition to the Church to "be ready" would have been ineffective as a spur to remain faithful.

Although I, as well as nearly all serious students of the Bible, have always held to the "can't-date" idea, I can no longer find any biblical basis for that belief. **A biblical prohibition to know exact dates for end-time events does not seem to exist.**

---

[b] I Corinthians 15:51, 52

CHAPTER 15
ERRONEOUS DATES

"Ah yes," some say, "Don't you remember that fanatics have forever been trying to date the Rapture, and they've always been wrong?"

It's true. They have all been wrong, but that in no way is a logical proof that we should not search the Scriptures on this subject.

Many people in past history tried to fly. Onlookers laughed while the believers in flight tried different methods and failed. The inventors persevered, and as we now know, they discovered the secrets of flight. Past failure or previous incorrect deductions concerning dates for end-time events, does not prove that the dates can never be discovered.

The Jews have also struggled with the precarious position on "date setting." In fact, the Talmud refers to leading rabbis who were frustrated with those who tried to calculate the coming of Messiah. It seems many students were anxious to study the prophetic dates in Daniel in order to discover the time for the coming of Messiah. The rabbis harshly warned that no one would be allowed to study and set a date, for the appearing of Messiah. "Blast the bones of the end-time calculators. For when they say such-and-such time and it does not come, the people despair and say: 'It's never going to come.'"[103]

They indicate that the avoidance of studying specific dates given to them by God grew out of a desire to shield their followers from possible disappointment. Their perceived importance of never making a mistake appeared to be of greater value to them than the study of the prophetic Scriptures God had given them concerning the coming Messiah! I wonder if they ever questioned why the Lord incorporated the dates in the Scriptures?

How tragic! If the Jews had counted the days given to them in the book of Daniel, they could have welcomed Jesus into the city on the day of His triumphal entry.

The Scripture in Daniel 9:25, 26, states,"*From the going forth of the commandment to restore and build Jerusalem unto the Messiah the prince shall be seven weeks, and threescore and two weeks...and after threescore and two weeks shall Messiah be cut off.*"

In *Daniel*, J. Vernon McGee writes concerning an Old Testament prophecy telling of the coming Messiah, "I feel that the decree of Artaxerxes in the twentieth year of his reign (Nehemiah 2:1−8) meets the requirements of Daniel 9:25. The commandment to rebuild the city of Jerusalem was issued in the month, Nisan, 445 B.C. That then will be our starting point.

"The first seven weeks of forty-nine years bring us to 397 B.C. and to Malachi and the end of the Old Testament. These were 'troublous times,' as witnessed to by both Nehemiah and Malachi.

"Sixty-two weeks, or 434 years, bring us to the Messiah... On this day Jesus rode into Jerusalem, offering Himself for the first time, publicly and officially, as the Messiah."[104]

Regrettably, the Jews chose not to study a portion of the Scriptures in order to insure their own credibility!

Even sadder yet, I hear those same words echoed today. "What if we are wrong? What if we calculate the wrong date? Nobody would believe us any more. We cannot afford to lose our credibility, you know." It appears at times that the fear of proposing an incorrect date has canceled out the study of God's intricately-woven prophetic time patterns in the Bible.

How amazing! We in the twentieth century still seem more concerned with what people think of us than with pursuing God-given information. Are we wise in choosing not to study portions of God's Word that might reveal the time of the soon coming Rapture?

The warning contained in Revelation 3:3 might apply to this mindset. *"Remember therefore how thou hast received and heard, and hold fast, and repent. If therefore thou shalt not watch, I will come on thee as a thief, and thou shalt not know what hour I will come upon thee."*

Jesus is telling us here that we are **to know** the hour of His coming.

How Then We Should Live

I now believe, as many others do, that it is possible to date the Rapture. If the times suggested in this writing, as to when the Rapture might occur, prove incorrect, the search will continue. As the true Rapture date draws near, I'm sure all students of the Word will see more clearly.

For now I have found, as a Christian, that the study of end-time prophecies causes me to apply more meaningfully the words of Ephesians 5:16, *"redeeming the time because the days are evil."*

The scriptural study of prophecy, makes real the words of God, as stated in Titus 2:13: *"Looking for that blessed hope, and the glorious appearing of the great God and our Savior Jesus Christ."*

Personal Reactions to Prophecy

If reading about prophecy and the end of civilization as we know it today, has put a scare into you, perhaps God is speaking to you. We have seen in this book that the atoning sacrifice of Jesus Christ is a truth that is presented throughout the whole Bible. Have you ever placed your faith in God's perfect Lamb, Jesus Christ? The familiar words of John 3:16 explain the plan God designed for you. *"For God so loved the world, that he gave his only begotton son, that whosoever believeth in him should not perish, but have everlasting life."*

Jesus is indeed the *"Lamb of God which taketh away the sin of the world."*[a] God explains again[b] that access to Him is gained solely on the basis of our faith in Jesus, never on any human effort or works. *"For by grace are ye saved through faith; and that not of yourselves: it is the gift of God; not of works lest any man should boast."*

God said to look forward to the coming Rapture of believers. He promised this would be a **comforting** experience for us. If you ask God to make Jesus **your** savior, then the loving words of comfort offered to believers in Jesus Christ will be yours. Don't wait any longer to make this commitment. Time is running out for all of us.

---

[a] John 1:29

[b] Ephesians 2:8,9

CONCLUSION
Is Prophecy a Waste of Time?

Some Christians, after considering the possibility of **knowing** the actual date, respond, "Why should I waste my time on studying prophecy or looking for some specific date? My concern is winning souls and living a godly life. Knowing an exact date wouldn't change my lifestyle, so why take the time?"

Giving these dedicated believers the benefit of the doubt, let's agree they are actually living every day of their life as if Jesus might come that very day. (Truthfully I have not met an abundance of this kind of Christian.) Still, most believers I know have many long-term plans that would not be in effect if they actually **knew** a close date that Jesus was going to come for them.

Certainly, if we don't have a definite date, we need both long and short-term plans. However, no matter how dedicated we might be, if we were to see a definite date outlined in the Bible, then surely the tempo and choices in our lives would be affected.

Almost two thousand years ago, the miracle birth of Jesus occurred. The Bible mentions two groups of informed people. Both of these groups knew prophecy. They knew the Scriptures that foretold the long hoped-for Messiah would be born in Bethlehem. But, both groups reacted differently to these Scriptures. One group, the wise men, saw "*His star in the East*" and came to worship Him. The other group, made up of religious leaders and Bible transcribers, quoted the Scriptures about His promised city of birth, **but they didn't even go to look to see if Messiah had really come.**[a] Today, let us be in the group of the wise men.

We must be very careful in stating what we **will or will not** study in the Scriptures. How bold it is of us to decide not to study certain biblical subjects saying, "It won't affect my life-style so why bother?" If we are not prohibited from searching the Scriptures for exact dates, and if those dates are there, they were put there by God, Himself. They were put there for us. They were put there to study. They were put there to discover at the appointed time.

Alas, as with many new thoughts, some readers will probably react with, "I can't give you an exact Scripture, but I still believe you can't know," or, "Sure, I can see it's not prohibited to date the Rapture, but knowing the exact date just doesn't interest me."

The excitement of studying God's word concerning prophetic timing is frustratingly difficult to share. No one enjoys the possibility of being "branded" by fellow believers. It would be much easier to tuck these questions and observations in an obscure place and continue with the majority's approach to this subject.

My heart's desire is to serve the Lord and honor Him by believing sound doctrine. This information is prepared for the body of Christ to ponder and critique. With great sincerity, my hope is that either the error of these observations will be **scripturally** rejected, or that these thoughts will excite others to further study along these lines.

What is your belief concerning the applications of Scriptures in this book?

---

[a] Matthew 2:1-10

When is the Rapture?

After you worked your way through all this information you didn't find my chosen date for the Rapture, did you? That's because I do not yet know the date.[b] Certainly there is strong evidence from the Jewish feasts for the Rapture to occur on some Rosh HaShanah, but still we don't know the year.

However, I hope after reading, studying, and praying about the information in this book you, too, will feel that the prohibition "to know," **does not exist.** When many believers begin to prayerfully search the Scriptures, I believe God will be true to His promise in John 16:13, *"Howbeit when he, the Spirit of truth, is come, he will guide you into all truth: for he shall not speak of himself; but whatsoever he shall hear, that shall he speak: and He will show you things to come."*

---

[b] I, as many others, have some possible ideas for the date of the Rapture. But they are just that, possible dates. It does not seem proper to include yet unsolidified possibilities in this book.

GLOSSARY

Hebrew words are denoted by an asterisk. Hebrew months are denoted by double asterisks.

Months are listed using the original order as given by God placing Abib (Nisan) as the first month.

Since the letters of the Hebrew alphabet are unique to their language, English versions of Hebrew words often are seen with more than one spelling.

Abib**	Original name of the first Hebrew calendar month Nisan.
Adar**	Twelfth month of the Hebrew calendar.
Antichrist	Satan-led man who will govern the world during a future seven-year period.
apostasy	A falling away from godly truth into gross error.
Aaron	Brother of Moses and chosen by God to be the first high priest. All priests came from his descendants.
Av**	Fifth month of the Hebrew calendar.

Azazel*	The Yom Kippur goat upon whose head the sins of the Jewish nation were placed.
Bikkurim*	Hebrew for Firstfruits which is also the celebration day of Jesus' Resurrection.
Chinuch*	Hebrew commentary of the Bible.
Church Age	Theological term for the expanse of time from the Day of Pentecost to the Rapture.
Elul**	Sixth month of the Hebrew calendar.
Erev Yom Kippur*	The evening before the actual day of Yom Kippur.
exegesis	A critical explanation of a portion of Scripture.
Gedaliah* (fast of)	A fast held on the third day of Tishri beginning the "Days of Awe."
Gentile	Any person who is not a Jew.
Gregorian Calendar	An A.D. 1582 adaptation of the calendar which had been introduced by Julius Caesar in 46 B.C. (Julian Calendar).
Hag-Ha Matzot*	Feast of Unleavened Bread which begins with the partaking of the Passover meal on Nisan 15.
Hallel*	Praise, especially referring to Psalms 113–118.

Heshvan**   Eighth month of the Hebrew calendar.

high priest   Jewish priest appointed as head of all the priests. He represented the nation during the annual entrance into the Holy of Holies.

homiletics   The art of preaching.

Holy of Holies   The inner room of the tabernacle (and later the temple). It was 10 x 10 x 10 cubits (a cube-shaped room of about fifteen foot depth, width, and height). It contained only The Ark of the Covenant. No one entered this windowless chamber except for the high priest on The Day of Atonement (Yom Kippur).

Huppah*   Final half of the wedding ceremony so named from the "huppah" canopy under which the bride and groom stand to be married by the rabbi.

Incarnation   A theological term referring to the appearance of God in the body of a man (Jesus Christ).

Imminence   A theological term for the "at any moment" expected calling-up of the Church by Jesus Christ.

Iyar**   Second month of the Hebrew calendar.

Kislev**   Ninth year of the Hebrew calendar.

Kohen*	A priest. (All must be a male descendants of the priestly line of Aaron.)
Levi*	One of Jacob's twelve sons. His descendants were called the "priestly" tribe and from them came Aaron.
liturgy	The public rites and services of the Christian Church.
Messiah*	The promised redeemer.
messianic*	Having to do with the Messiah.
Millennium	Theological term for the thousand-year time of peace yet to come in the future (Zechariah 14:9–21; Revelation 20:1–7).
Nisan**	First month of the Hebrew calendar. This is the religious calendar order as originally given by God.
Paschal*	Pertaining to Passover.
Pentecost	Feast of Weeks (the fiftieth day after Firstfruits or Resurrection).
Pesach*	Passover.
priest	One who officiates from man to God. In Judaism he must be a man from the tribe of Levi and a descendant of Aaron.
rabbi*	A teacher of the Jewish religion.

Rapture	The snatching away of believers by Jesus Christ.
Rosh HaShanah*	Feast of the Trumpets celebrated on Tishri 1.
Sabbath	The seventh day of the Jewish week counted from sundown to sundown. Corresponds to the Gentile's Friday night and Saturday day. "Sabbos" is the spelling used by most Jews.
Second Coming	The bodily return of Jesus Christ.
Shabbat*	The Sabbath before the Day of Atonement.
Shuvah Shavuot*	Feast of the fiftieth day after Firstfruits, also known as Pentecost.
Shiddukhin*	The arrangements and announcement of an engagement for marriage.
shofar*	A trumpet which is usually made from a ram's horn and sometimes from another clean animal's horn but never from metal.
Silvan**	Third month of the Hebrew calendar.
Succoth*	Feast of the Tabernacles or Booths which begins on Tishri 15.
tabernacle	Tent for sacrificial observances, designed by God and built during Moses' time.

Tabernacles	Referring to the week long feast of Succoth which begins on Tishri 15.
Talmud*	Jewish commentaries on the Tanakh or Old Testament.
Tamuz**	Fourth month of the Jewish calendar.
temple	First permanent worship structure built in Jerusalem for sacrificial observances. This temple, built by Solomon in 1004 B.C., was pillaged and left in disrepair by 640 B.C. It was gradually rebuilt and used until Herod began his grandiose version of the temple in 19 B.C. The Romans completely leveled his temple in A.D. 70, and no temple has been built on the site since then.
Tevet**	Tenth month of the Hebrew calendar.
Tishri**	Seventh month of the Hebrew calendar.
Torah*	The first five books of the Hebrew Bible. This term is often used when referring to the whole Jewish Bible (Old Testament).
Tribulation	A biblical term for the seven-year period of severe judgment from God upon the unbelieving population of the earth. This time begins with a pseudo peace led by the Antichrist, but ends in the worst time of judgment the world has ever known.

Yom Kippur*   Feast called The Day of Atonement, held
                   on Tishri 10.

Yom Teruah*   Day of Sounding the Horn; biblical
                   name for Rosh HaShanah from
                   Numbers 29:1.

BIBLIOGRAPHY

Agnon, S.Y. *Days of Awe.* New York: Schocken Books, 1948.

Alnor, William M. *Soothsayers of The Second Advent.* Old Tappan, N.J.: Power Books, 1989.

Barnhouse, Donald Grey. *Genesis.* Grand Rapids, MI: Zondervan Publishing House, 1970.

Berry, George Ricker. *Interlinear Greek – English New Testament.* Grand Rapids, MI: Baker Book House, 1987, 1989.

Burgess, Edward. *Christ: The Crown of The Torah.* Grand Rapids, MI: Zondervan Publishing House, 1986.

Bloch, Abraham P. *The Biblical and Historical Background of The Jewish Holy Days.* New York: KTAV Publishing House, Inc., 1978.

Buksbazen, Victor. *The Gospel in the Feasts of Israel.* Fort Washington, PA: Christian Literature Crusade, Inc., 1954.

Church, J.R. *The High Holy Days.* Oklahoma City: Southwest Radio Church, 1980.

Civelli, Joseph. *The Messiah's Return.* Nashville, TN: World Bible Society, 1988.

Daniel, Carey L. *The Bible's Seeming Contradictions.* Grand Rapids, MI: Zondervan Publishing House, 1941.

Davis John J. *Paradise to Prison.* Grand Rapids, MI: Baker Book House, 1975.

Davis, Leonard J. *Myths and Facts.* Washington, DC: Near East Report, 1989.

Deal, Colin. *The Day and the Hour Jesus Will Return.* Nashville, TN: World Bible Society, 1989.

Encyclopedia Judaica. Jerusalem: Keter Publishing House, 1972.

Edersheim, Alfred. *The Life and Times of Jesus the Messiah.* Peabody, MA: Hendrickson Publishers, 1883.

Evans, Mike. *Israel: America's Key To Survival.* Bedford, TX: Bedford Books, 1983.

Freeman, James M. *Manners and Customs of The Bible.* Plainfield, NJ: Logos International, 1972.

Fuchs, Daniel. *Israel's Holy Days.* Neptune, NJ: Loizeaux Brothers, 1985.

Gaebelein, Arno C. *The Gospel of Matthew.* Neptune, NJ: Loizeaux Brothers, 1961.

Gaster, Theodor. *Festivals of the Jewish New Year.* New York: William Morrow Co., 1952.

Glaser, Mitch and Zhava. *The Fall Feasts of Israel.* Chicago: Moody Press, 1987.

Goodman, Philip. *The Passover Anthology*. Philadelphia: The Jewish Publication Society of America, 1961.

Goodman, Philip. *The Rosh HaShanah Anthology*. Philadelphia: The Jewish Publication Society of America, 1970.

Goodman, Philip. *The Shavuot Anthology*. Philadelphia: The Jewish Publication Society of America, 1974.

Goodman, Philip. *The Sukkot and Simhat Anthology*. Philadelphia: The Jewish Publication Society of America, 1988.

Goodman, Philip. *The Yom Kippur Anthology*. Philadephia, : The Jewish Publication Society of America, 1971.

Good, Joseph. *Rosh HaShanah and the Messianic Kingdom to Come*. Port Arthur, TX: Hatikva Ministries, 1989.

Gross, David C. *The Jewish People's Almanac*. New York: Hippocrene Books, 1981.

Habershon, Ada R. *Types in The Old Testament*. Grand Rapids, MI: Kregel Publications, 1988.

Harevueni, Nogah. *Nature in Our Biblical Heritage*. Kiryat Ono, Israel: Neot Kedumim Ltd.

Henry, Matthew. *Commentaries of Genesis to Deuteronomy and Matthew to John*. Old Tappan, NJ: Flemming H. Revell Company.

The Holy Bible: Authorized King James Version. Nashville: Thomas Nelson, Inc., 1976.

Ironside, Harry A. *Matthew*. Neptune, NJ: Loizeaux Brothers, 1948.

Israel My Glory. Vol. 48. No. 3. Bellmawr, NJ: The Friends of Israel Gospel Ministry, Inc., 1990.

Jeffrey, Grant R. *Heaven: The Last Frontier*. Toronto, Ontario: Frontier Research Publications, 1990.

Jeffrey, Grant R. *Armageddon Appointment With Destiny*. Toronto, Ontario: Frontier Research Publications, 1988.

The Jewish Publication Society. *Tanakh* The New JPS Translation. Philadelphia: 1988.

Jones, Vendyl. *The Search for the Ashes of the Red Heifer*. Oklahoma City: Southwest Radio Church, 1981.

Kac, Arthur W. *The Messianic Hope*. Grand Rapids, MI: Baker Book House, 1974.

Kac, Arthur W. *The Messiahship of Jesus*. Grand Rapids, MI: Baker Book House, 1980.

Kieval, Herman. *The High Holy Days: Book One: Rosh Hashanah*. New York: The Burning Book Press, 1959.

Lang, John Peter. *Commentary on the Holy Scriptures: Exodus and Leviticus*. Grand Rapids, MI: Zondervan Publishing Company.

Leibowitz, Nehama. *Studies in Bramidbar Numbers*. Jerusalem: World Zionist Organization, 1980.

Lewis, David Allen. *Prophecy 2000*. Green Forest, AZ: New Leaf Press, 1990.

Lindsey, Hal. *The Road to Holocaust*. New York: Bantam Books, 1989.

Lindsey, Hal. *The Late Great Planet Earth*. Grand Rapids, MI: Zondervan Publishing House, 1970.

Lippel. *The Book of Feasts in the Holy Land Israel*. Jerusalem: Institute Of Interreligious Relations And Research, 1982.

Litvin, Danny. *Pentecost Is Jewish*. Orange, CA: Promise Publishing, 1987.

McGee, J. Vernon. *Exodus 1975, Leviticus 1975, Matthew 1973, Mark 1975, Luke 1975, John 1976, Hebrews 1978*. Pasadena, CA: Thru The Bible Radio.

McGee, J. Vernon. *The Tabernacle: God's Portrait of Christ*. Pasadena, CA: Thru the Bible Radio, 1970.

Ministry of Foreign Affairs. *Facts About Israel*. Jerusalem: Information Division, 1979.

Neusner, Jacob. *Invitation to The Talmud*. San Francisco: Harper and Row, 1973.

Neusner, Jacob. *Invitation to The Midrash*. San Francisco: Harper and Row, 1989.

Pentecost, Dwight J. *Things to Come*. Grand Rapids, MI: Zondervan Publishing House, 1978.

Pettingill, William L. *Bible Questions Answered*. Grand Rapids, MI: Zondervan Publishing House, 1965.

Pink, Arthur W. *Gleanings in Exodus*. Chicago: Moody Press, 1972.

Pulpit Commentary, The. Peabody, MA: Hendrickson Publishers.

Rausch, David A. *Building Bridges.* Chicago: Moody Press, 1988.

Rosen, Ceil and Moishe. *Christ in the Passover.* Chicago, IL: Moody Press, 1978.

Shepherd, Coulson. *Jewish Holy Days.* Neptune, NJ: Loizeaux Brothers, 1961.

Showers, Regnald E. *Behold the Bridegroom Comes.* Bellmawr, NJ: The Friends of Israel Gospel Ministry.

Steinberg, Milton. *Basic Judaism.* New York: Harvest/HBJ Book.

Strauss, Lehman. *God's Prophetic Calendar.* Neptune, NJ: Loizeaux Brothers, 1987.

Spence, Very Rev. H. D. M. and Rev. Joseph S. Exell. *The Pulpit Commentary: Exodus Vols I and II.* New York: Funk and Wagnalls Company.

Taylor, Charles R. *Get All Excited Jesus Is Coming Soon!* Redondo Beach, CA: Today in Bible Prophecy, 1974.

Taylor, Charles R. *Watch World Events.* Nashville: World Bible Society, 1989.

Stern, David H. *Jewish New Testament.* Jerusalem: Jewish New Testament Publications, 1989.

Walvoord, John F. *Matthew Thy Kingdom Come.* Chicago: Moody Press, 1974.

Walvoord, John F. *The Rapture Question*. Grand Rapids, MI: Zondervan Publishing House, 1979.

Walvrood, John F. *The Revelation of Jesus Christ*. Chicago: Moody Press, 1966.

Waskow, Arthur. *Seasons of Our Joy*. New York: Bantam Books, 1982.

Werblowsky, R.J., Zwi and Geoffrey W. Goder, eds. *Encyclopedia of The Jewish Religion*. Israel: Massada PGC Press LTD, 1965.

Wiersbe, Warren W. *Be God's Guest: Feasts of Leviticus 23*. Lincoln, NB: Back to the Bible Broadcast, Victor Books, 1982.

Wolpin, Rabbi Nisson, ed. *Seasons of The Soul*. Agudath, Israel: Mesorah Publications Ltd., 1981.

Josephus, The Works of. Peabody, MA: Hendrickson Publishers, 1987.

ENDNOTES

1. William A. Alnor, *Soothsayers of the Second Advent* (Old Tappan, New Jersey: Power Books, Fleming Revell Company Publishers 1989), p. 58.

2. Mircea Eliade, ed., *The Encyclopedia of Religion* (New York: MacMillan Publishing Co. 1987), vol. 9., p. 530.

3. John Elson, "Essay" *Time* (February 11, 1991), p. 88.

4. Jeffery L. Sheler, "A Revelation in the Middle East" *US News and World Report* (November 19, 1990), pp. 67-68.

5. James Hastings, ed., *The Encyclopedia of Religion and Ethics* (New York: Charles Scribner's Son), vol. 11., p. 284.

6. Ibid. vol. 11., p. 285.

7. Ron Rhodes, "Millennial Madness" *Christian Research Journal* (Fall 1990), p. 39.

8. Hastings, op. cit. pp. 285-286.

9. *L'Accomplissement des propheties, ou la deliverance prechaine de l'eglise* (Rotterdam 1686), 2 vols.

10. Hastings, op. cit. p. 286.

11. David Allen Lewis, *Prophecy 2000* (Green Forest, Arizona: New Leaf Press, 1990), p. 222.

12. Grant Jeffrey, *Heaven The Last Frontier* (Frontier Research Publications, 1990), pp. 93-118.

13. *Jerusalem Post* (September 1, 1990).

14. "Spotlight", (*Jerusalem Post*, March 9, 1991).

15. *Encyclopedia Judaica* (Jerusalem: Keter Publishing House 1972), vol. 11., p. 1031.

16. Ibid.

17. James M. Freeman, *Manners and Customs of the Bible* (Plainfield, New Jersey: Logos, 1972), p. 330.

18. *Encyclopedia Judaica* vol. 11., op. cit. p. 1031.

19. Freeman, op. cit. p. 376.

20. Charles F. Pfeiffer, Howard F. Vos and John Rea *The Wycliffe Bible Encyclopedia* (Chicago: Moody Press 1975), p. 1082.

21. *Encyclopedia Judaica* vol. 11., op. cit. p. 1034.

22. George E. Ladd, *The Blessed Hope* pp. 99–102.

23. Coulson Shepherd, *Jewish Holy Days* (Neptune, New Jersey: Loizeaux Brothers 1961) p. 11.

24. Exodus 12:2, Leviticus 23:4, 5

25. Interestingly each plague demonstrated God's supremacy over the chief deities of Egypt. *See* J. Vernon McGee's opening notes for Exodus in his *Thru the Bible* version of the Bible for a detailed account of Egypt's defeated gods.

26. Abraham P. Bloch, *The Biblical and Historical Background of The Jewish Holy Days* (Jerusalem: KTAV Publishing House Ltd, 1978), p. 107.

27. Edward Burgess, *Christ: The Crown of the Torah* (Grand Rapids, MI: Zondervan Publishing House, 1986), pp. 88-89.

28. Josephus, *The Works of Josephus* "Wars of the Jews" (Peabody, MA: Hendrickson Publishers, Inc., 1987), Book 6/ Chapter 9/3.

29. Arthur W. Pink, *Gleanings in Genesis* (Chicago: Moody Press, 1922), pp. 170-171.

30. Lehman Strauss, *God's Prophetic Calendar* (Neptune, New Jersey: Loizeaux Brothers, 1987), pp. 28-29.

31. J. D. Douglas, ed., *The New Bible Dictionary* (Grand Rapids MI: Wm. B. Eerdmans Publishing Co., 1962), pp. 1209-1210.

32. J. Vernon McGee, *Exodus* (Pasadena, CA: Thru The Bible Radio, 1975), vol. I., pp. 99-100. Arthur W. Pink, *Gleanings in Exodus* (Chicago: Moody Press, 1922), p. 90.

33. Bloch, op. cit. p. 103.

34. Alfred Edersheim, *The Life and Times of Jesus the Messiah* (Peabody MA: Hendrickson Publishers, 1883), p. 490.
     Encyclopedia Judaica vol. 13., op. cit. p. 170.

35. *Encyclopedia Judaica* vol. 12., op. cit. p. 22.

36. Ibid. vol. 14 p. 611.

37. Ibid. vol. 14., p. 613.

38. ibid. vol. 13., p. 171.

39. Josephus, loc. cit.

40. Pink, op. cit. p. 93.

41. Bloch, op. cit. pp. 108-109.

42. Daniel Fuchs, *Israel's Holy Days in Type and Prophecy* (Neptune, New Jersey: Loizeaux Brothers, 1985), p. 29.

43. *Encyclopedia Judaica* vol. 14., op. cit. p. 1319.
Zwi R. J. Werblowsky and Geoffrey Wigoder, ed. *Encyclopedia of Jewish Religion* (Masada PEC Press Ltd., 1965), p. 401.

44. Victor Buksbazen, *The Gospel in the Feasts of Israel* (Fort Washington, PA: 1954 Christian Literature Crusade, 1954), p. 18.

45. *The Scofield Reference Bible* (Oxford University Press Inc. 1909), p. 156.

46. Bloch, op. cit. p. 185.

47. Bloch, op. cit. p. 188.
Danny Litvin, *Pentecost Is Jewish* (Orange, CA: Promise Publishing, 1987), pp. 14-15.

48. Litvin, loc. cit.

49. Ibid. pp. 44-48.

50. Jeremiah 5:24; Hosea 5:12-6:3; Joel 2:23; Zechariah 10:1; James 5:7,8

51. In considering this thought we must first note, according to *The New Bible Dictionary* p.856 Eerdmans 1962, "The meaning of the term "mysterion" in classical Greek is 'anything hidden or secret' ... In the New Testament "mysterion" signifies a secret which is being, or even has been, revealed, which is also divine in scope, and needs to be made known by God to men through His Spirit."
The prevailing theological interpretation is that "mystery" in Scripture is a previously hidden truth, now divinely revealed. (*see* old Scofield Bible notes, Matt. 13 # 3).
Some apply this definition of "not being revealed" to mean that "mysteries" are not even referred to in the scriptures before the time of their unveiling. This belief leads to statements such as "The Church is not included in the feasts of Israel." This conclusion, based on the use of "mystery," seems inaccurate since some of the twenty-five N.T. appearances of "mystery/mysteries" describe subjects which have their first appearance in the Old Testament. For example, notice the I Timothy 3:16 "mystery" reference of the pre-existence, incarnation and work of Jesus yet, almost the whole book of Hebrews unveils the **prefigurements of Jesus in the tabernacle and Old Testament types.**

Could God be calling these subjects "mysteries" until their unveiling by the Holy Spirit because up until their disclosure, they were yet to be understood?

52. Bloch, op. cit. p. 196.

53. Ibid.

54. *Encyclopedia Judaica* vol. 14., op. cit. p. 1444.

55. Theodor Gaster, *Festivals Of The Jewish Year* (William Morrow & Co., 1952), p. 113.
    Herman Kieval, *The High Holy Days* (New York, NY: The Burning Bush Press, 1959), p. 120.

56. Isaac Klein, *A Guide To Jewish Practices* (New York, NY: The Jewish Theological Seminary of America, 1979), p. 196.

57. Joseph Civelli, *The Messiah's Return* (Nashville: World Bible Society, 1983), p. 37.

58. S. Y. Agnon, *Days Of Awe* (New York, NY: Schoken Books 1948), pp. 79-80.

59. Herman Kieval, *The High Holy Days* (New York, NY: Burning Bush Press, 1959) Book One: Rosh HaShanah p. 109.

60. Bloch, op. cit. p. 25.

61. Joseph Good, *"The Akeida - Binding of the Sacrifice"* Tape series. (Port Arthur, TX: Hatikva Ministries), series st 4.

62. Bloch, op. cit. p. 21.

63. Rabbi Ishmael (2nd century) quoted in Bloch, op. cit. pp. 23-24.

64. Bloch, op. cit. p. 24.

65. Buksbazen, op. cit. p.25.

66. Scofield Reference Bible, 1909 edition, "The Feast of Trumpets", Leviticus 23: 23-25, note # 2, p. 157.

67. *Jerusalem Post* March 16 1991 p.1.

68. Bloch, op. cit. p.16.

69. Ibid. p. 24.

70. *Encyclopedia Judaica* vol. 5., op. cit. p. 1382.

71. Buksbazen, op. cit. p. 41.

72. Bloch, op.cit. p. 34.

73. Ibid. p. 34.

74. Ibid. p. 37.

75. Buksbazen, op. cit. p. 36.

76. Agnon, op. cit. p. 148.

77. J. Vernon McGee, *The Tabernacle: God's Portrait of Christ* (Pasadena, CA: Thru The Bible Radio, 1937), p. 81.

78. Burgess, op. cit. p. 107.
Gaster, op. cit. pp. 146-147.

79. *Encyclopedia Judaica* vol. 15., op. cit p. 969.

80. Ibid. vol. 15., p. 978.

81. Agnon, op. cit. p.130.

82. Ibid.

83. Philip Goodman, *The Yom Kippur Anthology* (quote from Franz Rosenzweig) (Philadelphia: The Jewish Publication Society Of America, 1971), pp. 133-134.

84. Arthur Wascow, *Seasons of Our Joy* (New York: Bantam Books, 1982), p. 27.

85. From instructions in Numbers 29:12-39, each day two rams, fourteen lambs and one goat were offered. Interestingly, the first day thirteen young bullocks (bulls) were required and each day thereafter this number diminished by one.
      According to Arthur Wascow in *Seasons of Our Joy* p. 54, "The total number of seventy bullocks being offered was said by Rabbinic tradition to celebrate the seventy nations on earth...Thus during Succoth the people of Israel became priests on behalf of all the peoples without their consent — that they needed the help of the God of Heaven." (The number of seventy for the nations comes from Genesis chapter 10.)

86. Waskow, op. cit. p. 49-52.
Gaster, op. cit. pp. 80-83

87. Rabbi Ralph Pelcovitz, "Seasons of the Soul" (article) (Brooklyn, NY: Mesorah Publications, Ltd., 1969), p. 73.

88. Pelcovitz, Ibid.

89. Gaster, op. cit. p. 86.

90. Philip Goodman, *The Sukkot/Simhat Torah Anthology* (Philadelphia: The Jewish Publication Society, 1988), p. 43.

91. Charles J. Woodbridge, *Bible Prophecy* (Chicago: Moody Bible Institute 1962), p. 23.

92. Dwight J. Pentecost, *Things to Come* (Dunham Publishing Company, 1958/ Grand Rapids, MI: Zondervan Publishing Company), p. 229.

93. Even when the thief analogy is speaking of Jesus it typifies an unexpected appearance which brings about judgment to the unobservant slacker.
    The Rapture should be a "blessed hope" not a negative experience. There seems to be no scriptural justification to warrant the belief that Jesus will appear to obedient Christians as a thief. See Matthew 24:43, 26:55; Mark 14:48; Luke 12:33, 39, 22:52; John 10:1, 10:10, 12:6; I Thessalonians 5:2, 4; I Peter 4:15, II Peter 3:10, Revelation 3:3, 16:15

94. Harry A. Ironside, *Matthew* (Neptune, NJ: Loizeaux Brothers, 1948), p. 316.

95. Arno C. Gaebelein, *The Gospel Of Matthew* (Neptune, NJ: Loizeaux Brothers, 1910), p. 511.

96. John F. Walvoord, *Matthew Thy Kingdom Come* (Chicago: Moody Press, 1974), pp. 181, 191.

97. J. Vernon McGee, *Matthew* (Pasadena, CA: Thru The Bible Radio, 1973), vol. 2., p. 105.

98. John F. Walvrood, *The Rapture Question* (Grand Rapids, MI: Zondervan Publishing House, 1979), p. 189.

99. J. Vernon McGee, *Mark* (Pasadena, CA: Thru The Bible Books, 1975), p. 150.

100. Donald Grey Barnhouse, *Genesis* (Grand Rapids, MI: Zondervan Publishing House, 1970), p. 30.

101. J. Vernon McGee, *Hebrews* (Pasadena CA: Thru The Bible Books, 1978), vol. 2., p. 46.
The Pulpit Commentary (Peabody, MA: Hendrickson Publishers), vol. XXI., pp.241, 250, 262 and vol. XV p. 464
Walvoord, *Matthew* op.cit. pp. 191-104.

102. It is interesting to note the observations in *The Pulpit Commentary* vol. XV pp. 463,464. After a discussion on whether or not God reveals the future to believers, J. A. MacDonald comments, "Wisdom withholds particular revelations of the future to encourage prayer. Yet is it generally made known to the wise...The wise who study this series cannot be ignorant as to the approaching time. But to the wicked it will come as a surprise."

103. *Jerusalem Post*, (February 16, 1991), [Sanhedrin 97b].

104. J. Vernon McGee, *Daniel* (Pasadena, CA: Thru The Bible Books, 1978), pp. 156.